Fun Projects for You and the Kids

by DAVID

with illustration

THE LYO
AN IMPRINT OF THE
GUILFORD, C

TO MY SON
JAIME

The Lyons Press is an imprint of The Globe Pequot Press.

10 9 8 7 6 5 4 3 2 1

Printed in the United States of America
Designed by David Stiles

ISBN: 978-1-59921-189-3

Library of Congress Cataloging-in-Publication Data is available on file.

Disclaimer: David Stiles (the "Author") makes no express or implied representations or warranties, including warranties of performance, merchantability, and fitness for a particular purpose, regarding this information. Your use of this book is at your own risk. You assume full responsibility and risk of loss resulting from the use of this information. The Author will not be responsible for any direct special, indirect, incidental, consequential or punitive damages or any other damages whatsoever.

Note: Every effort has been made to design all the projects in this book to be safe and easy to build; however, it is impossible to predict every situation and the ability of each carpenter who builds them. Therefore, it is advised that the reader seek advice from a competent, on-site expert.

To buy books in quantity for corporate use
or incentives, call **(800) 962–0973**
or e-mail **premiums@GlobePequot.com**.

CONTENTS

TOOLS & MATERIALS

HOUSES

WATER FUN

INDOOR PROJECTS

OUTDOOR PROJECTS

ABOUT THIS BOOK

THIS book was conceived and designed to give the reader or handyman some ideas on projects for children. It is, therefore, essentially a book on **WHAT** to make rather than HOW to make it. It began several years ago in the form of pencil sketches that I did in my spare time in anticipation of the future, when my son would be old enough to enjoy these things. At that time I was not too old to remember the things I had built when I was a boy, or the things I wished I had made.

This book is intended to be an inspiration to the reader rather than a Bible to copy from. I have purposely omitted all but the most general dimensions and specifications, so that the reader will feel free to change any designs or details to his own liking or to meet his own requirements. Nothing is more frustrating than to follow step-by-step directions from a set of plans, only to find that your lumber yard doesn't carry this particular size wood or that dimension is too large to fit where you want it—and you end up changing the plans anyway. It is rare that any two people will make the same thing in the same way, because of the difference in available materials, tools, or skill. In all of the designs in this book I have attempted to offer at least one possible way in which the particular project could be made, wherever it seemed necessary. This is only a starting point, however, and the reader will probably want to make more detailed plans to meet his own needs. In all cases the projects were designed to be easily made at a minimum cost, using materials found around the house.

Types of finishes are generally left up to individual taste. It is suggested, however, that there should be a minimum of sanding and finishing. Avoid trying to copy "store toys" which are often painted bright, garish colors to make them sell better. It is often best to leave an object in its natural wood color. Flat stains, varnish, or shellac can often enhance and at the same time hide joints that don't quite fit. Remember, some of these projects might become permanent fixtures in your back yard, and you and your neighbors are going to have to live with them for a long time. Be careful of using paint. Paint chips, scratches, and always requires maintenance after several months of child-wear. The important thing is that the objects exist for the child's pleasure, and surface embellishments do little to achieve this purpose.

AUTHOR'S INTRODUCTION

WHAT has happened to the tree huts, the secret hiding places, the lemonade stands? Have they been forgotten in the wake of television, computers and Palm pilots? What has happened to all those wonderful things we grown-ups played with when we were young? Modern psychology has done much to teach our children to adjust socially and to mature quicker through organized and, all too often, "supervised" play. Children's books are today directed toward informative learning, toys are designed to be "assembled" without stimulation to the imagination, and in school, play has become competitive and overly-organized, restricting a child's creativity and almost putting an end to imaginative playtime. No wonder the young turn toward TV and video games.

What about Mom and Dad—how can they help? Working at an office or high pressured job all day, coming home tired, today's parents tend to spend less time with their children than in the past when life was simpler. This loss of quality, relaxed time, so important for families to share, was my main inspiration for writing this book. As parents, finding time to work on a special project with our kids, getting to know them better, is essential. Building projects together is just one of the ways in which this can be done. This time will be valued and remembered by your children, as they grow older. A father once told me that one of the most memorable moments he had spent with his child, was sitting in a tree, and planning how they would build a treehouse.

TOOLS

Here are a few basic tools and help-ful hints on how to use them.

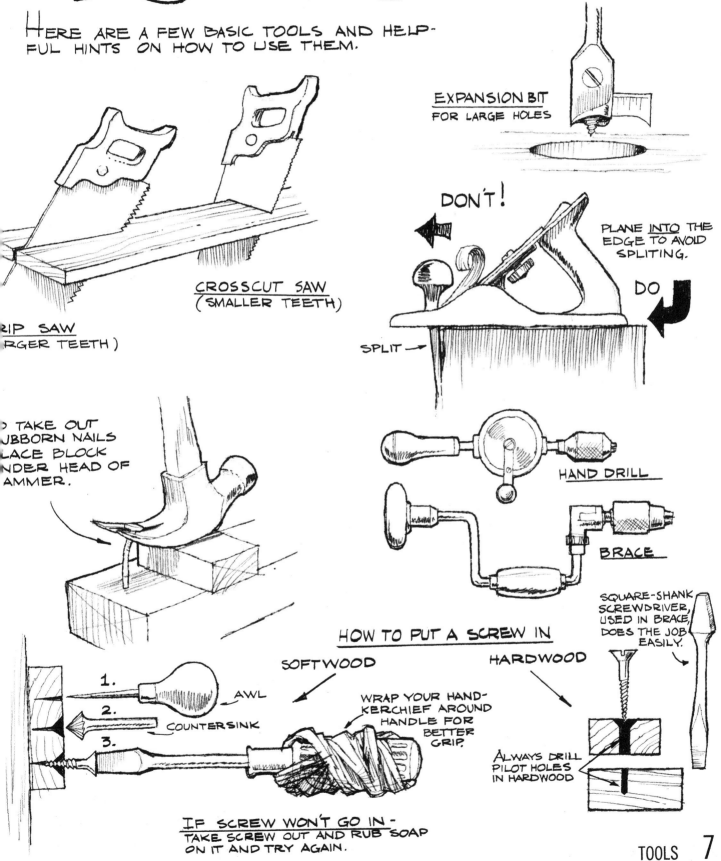

EXPANSION BIT
FOR LARGE HOLES

CROSSCUT SAW
(SMALLER TEETH)

RIP SAW
(LARGER TEETH)

DON'T!

PLANE INTO THE
EDGE TO AVOID
SPLITING.

DO

SPLIT →

TO TAKE OUT
STUBBORN NAILS
PLACE BLOCK
UNDER HEAD OF
HAMMER.

HAND DRILL

BRACE

SQUARE-SHANK
SCREWDRIVER,
USED IN BRACE,
DOES THE JOB
EASILY.

HOW TO PUT A SCREW IN

SOFTWOOD

HARDWOOD

1.
2.
3.

AWL
COUNTERSINK

WRAP YOUR HAND-
KERCHIEF AROUND
HANDLE FOR
BETTER
GRIP.

ALWAYS DRILL
PILOT HOLES
IN HARDWOOD

IF SCREW WON'T GO IN -
TAKE SCREW OUT AND RUB SOAP
ON IT AND TRY AGAIN.

MATERIALS

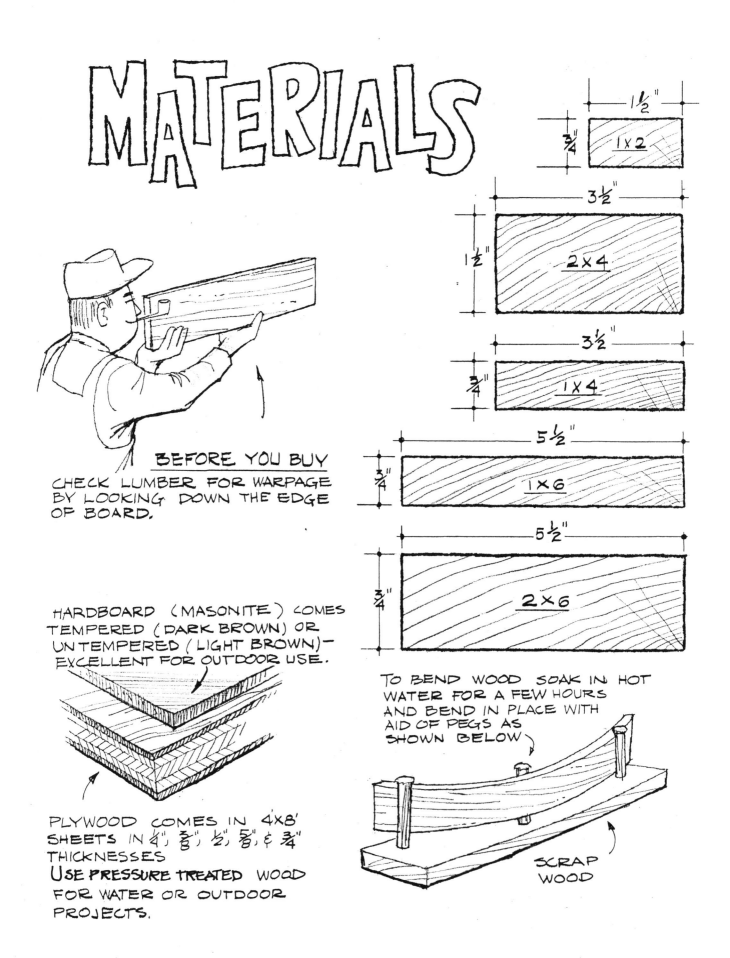

1½"

¾" 1X2

3½"

1½" 2X4

3½"

¾" 1X4

5½"

¾" 1X6

5½"

¾" 2X6

BEFORE YOU BUY

CHECK LUMBER FOR WARPAGE BY LOOKING DOWN THE EDGE OF BOARD.

HARDBOARD (MASONITE) COMES TEMPERED (DARK BROWN) OR UNTEMPERED (LIGHT BROWN)— EXCELLENT FOR OUTDOOR USE.

PLYWOOD COMES IN 4'X8' SHEETS IN ¼", ⅜", ½", ⅝", & ¾" THICKNESSES
USE PRESSURE TREATED WOOD FOR WATER OR OUTDOOR PROJECTS.

TO BEND WOOD SOAK IN HOT WATER FOR A FEW HOURS AND BEND IN PLACE WITH AID OF PEGS AS SHOWN BELOW

SCRAP WOOD

JOINTS

Always plan joints carefully before starting a project. Below are some examples of joints you might use.

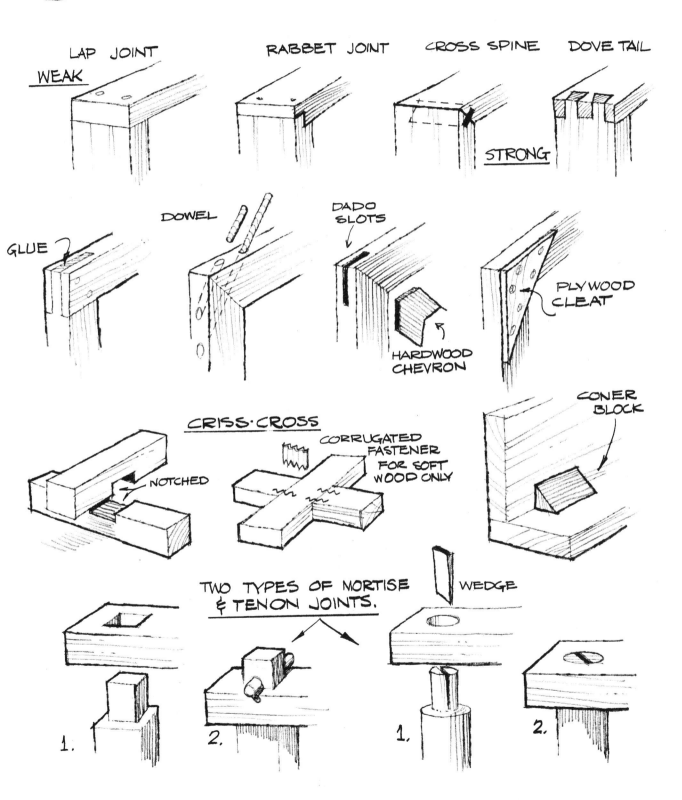

LAP JOINT — WEAK

RABBET JOINT

CROSS SPINE

DOVE TAIL — STRONG

GLUE

DOWEL

DADO SLOTS — HARDWOOD CHEVRON

PLYWOOD CLEAT

CRISS-CROSS — NOTCHED

CORRUGATED FASTENER FOR SOFT WOOD ONLY

CONER BLOCK

TWO TYPES OF MORTISE & TENON JOINTS.

WEDGE

1. 2.   1. 2.

NAILS - SCREWS - BOLTS

NAILS ARE GOOD

NAILS USED IN THE
WRONG APPLICATION
CAN PULL OUT EASILY

BAD
(PARALLEL TO
GRAIN)

GOOD
(RIGHT ANGLES
TO GRAIN)

BAD   GOOD
STAGGER NAILS
TO AVOID SPLITTING

COMMON NAIL

FINISHING NAIL

ROOFING NAIL

FLOORING NAIL

MASONRY NAIL

SCREWS ARE BETTER

FLAT   ROUND   OVAL   LAG

BOLTS ARE BEST

CARRIAGE
BOLT

SHOULDER KEEPS
BOLT FROM TURNING

WING
NUT

LAG
SCREW

MACHINE
BOLTS

HOUSES

HOUSES

THERE is something mysterious and wonderful about the eternal hut for children. Remember the summerhouse or the grape arbor where you played long hours on summer afternoons? A house for a child might be branches of a tree, a secret place under the bushes, a hole in the ground, or a big cardboard box; but a real playhouse is even more exciting. A house might become anything from an imagined miniature household to the most fantastic castle out of a fairy tale book. There is an element of excitement in having a house high in a tree where the owner can spy on imagined invaders, or just retreat from the world for a timeless moment on a summer day. A child's house can be a hundred different things in one day—it can change from a jungle hut to a fort, to a school, a hospital, and perhaps even to a spaceship. It's a good place to put dolls to sleep in, to keep pets from going out of, to hold secret meetings in or, occasionally, even to camp overnight. To a child, his or her house becomes an adventure—a secret place, which, most important is all their own, and where grown-ups need permission to enter.

TREE HUT

A TREE HUT DEPENDS LARGELY ON THE TYPES OF TREES AVAILABLE. THIS TREE HUT IS BUILT ON ONE TREE THAT HAS AT LEAST TWO BRANCHES AND THE TRUNK SUPPORTING THE CORNERS OF THE HOUSE. THE OTHER CORNER IS SUPPORTED BY BUILDING UP A STRUT FROM THE TRUNK. ALWAYS BEGIN BY BUILDING A STRONG PLATFORM. SINCE EVERY TREE IS DIFFERENT, IT IS DIFFICULT TO DESIGN THE HOUSE FIRST AND FIND A TREE TO FIT IT. IT IS BETTER TO FIND THE TREE AND LET IT SUGGEST THE FORM OF THE HOUSE, AS YOU WILL SEE IN THE FOLLOWING PAGES.

TRIANGLE TREE HUT

BUILT AROUND THREE TREES AT MORE OR LESS EQUAL DISTANCE FROM EACH OTHER.

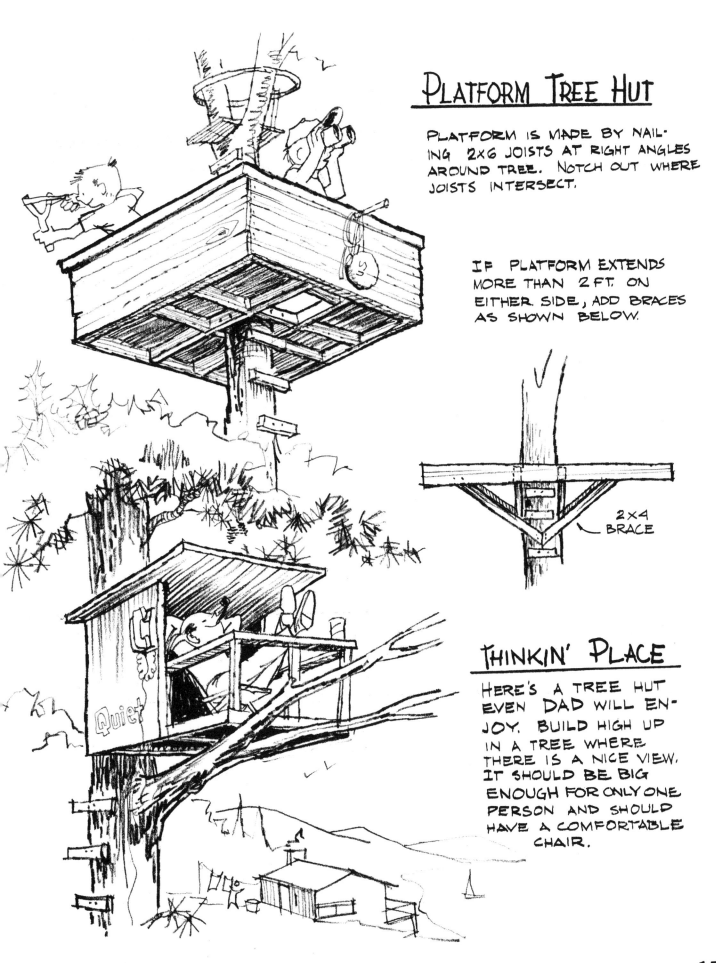

Platform Tree Hut

Platform is made by nailing 2x6 joists at right angles around tree. Notch out where joists intersect.

If platform extends more than 2 ft. on either side, add braces as shown below.

2x4 Brace

Thinkin' Place

Here's a tree hut even Dad will enjoy. Build high up in a tree where there is a nice view. It should be big enough for only one person and should have a comfortable chair.

FOUR POSTER

THIS TREE HOUSE IS MADE
FROM STRAIGHT LOGS, CUT
IN THE WOODS, AND DRAGGED
TO THE DESIRED LOCATION. THIS
SAVES TIME IN FINDING THE IDEAL
TREE OR GROUP OF TREES IN WHICH
TO MAKE THE TREE HUT.

HiLL HOUSE

LOOKOUT POST

FILL

COVER FLOOR &
BACK WITH LOGS
TO PERSERVE
DRYNESS

FLOOR

EXCAVATE

CROSS
SECTION

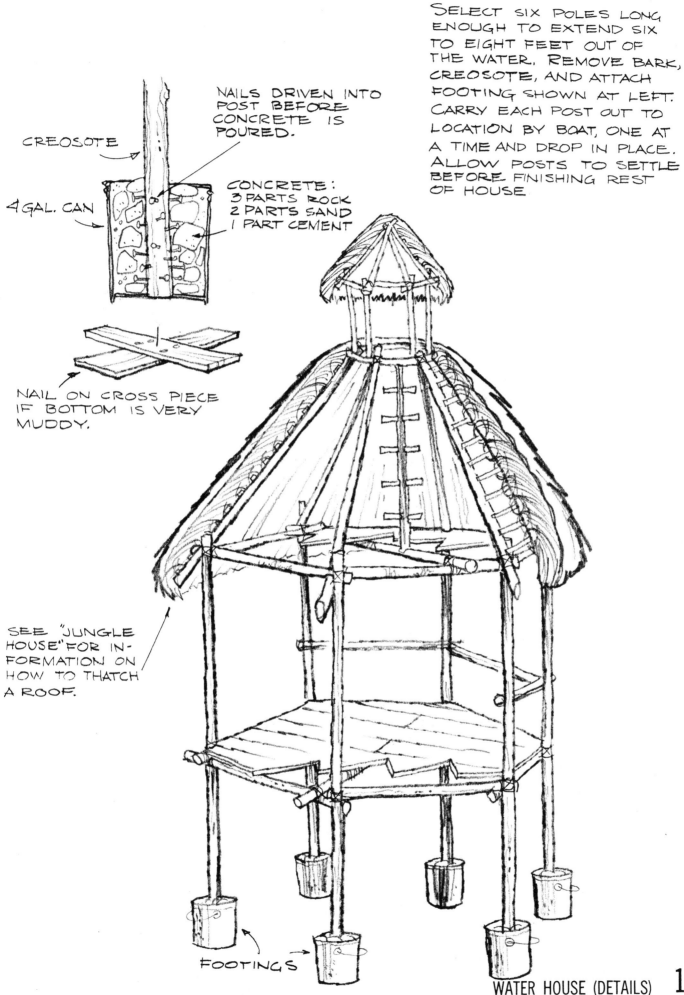

CREOSOTE

4 GAL. CAN

NAILS DRIVEN INTO POST BEFORE CONCRETE IS POURED.

CONCRETE:
3 PARTS ROCK
2 PARTS SAND
1 PART CEMENT

SELECT SIX POLES LONG ENOUGH TO EXTEND SIX TO EIGHT FEET OUT OF THE WATER. REMOVE BARK, CREOSOTE, AND ATTACH FOOTING SHOWN AT LEFT. CARRY EACH POST OUT TO LOCATION BY BOAT, ONE AT A TIME AND DROP IN PLACE. ALLOW POSTS TO SETTLE BEFORE FINISHING REST OF HOUSE.

NAIL ON CROSS PIECE IF BOTTOM IS VERY MUDDY.

SEE "JUNGLE HOUSE" FOR INFORMATION ON HOW TO THATCH A ROOF.

FOOTINGS

WATER HOUSE (DETAILS)

19

LOG CABIN

IF YOU LIVE IN AN AREA WHERE TALL STRAIGHT PINE TREES ARE AVAILABLE, THIS IS THE HOUSE FOR YOU. BE SURE YOU HAVE ABOUT 30 TREES AND LOTS OF TIME BEFORE YOU BEGIN. THIS TYPE OF HOUSE IS SLOW TO BUILD BECAUSE MOST OF THE WORK IS DONE BY AXE. USE AS FEW NAILS AS POSSIBLE AND AS LITTLE CUT LUMBER AS POSSIBLE. A HOUSE OF THIS KIND IS A RARITY THESE DAYS AND BECOMES A REWARDING EXPERIENCE WHEN YOU FINISH.

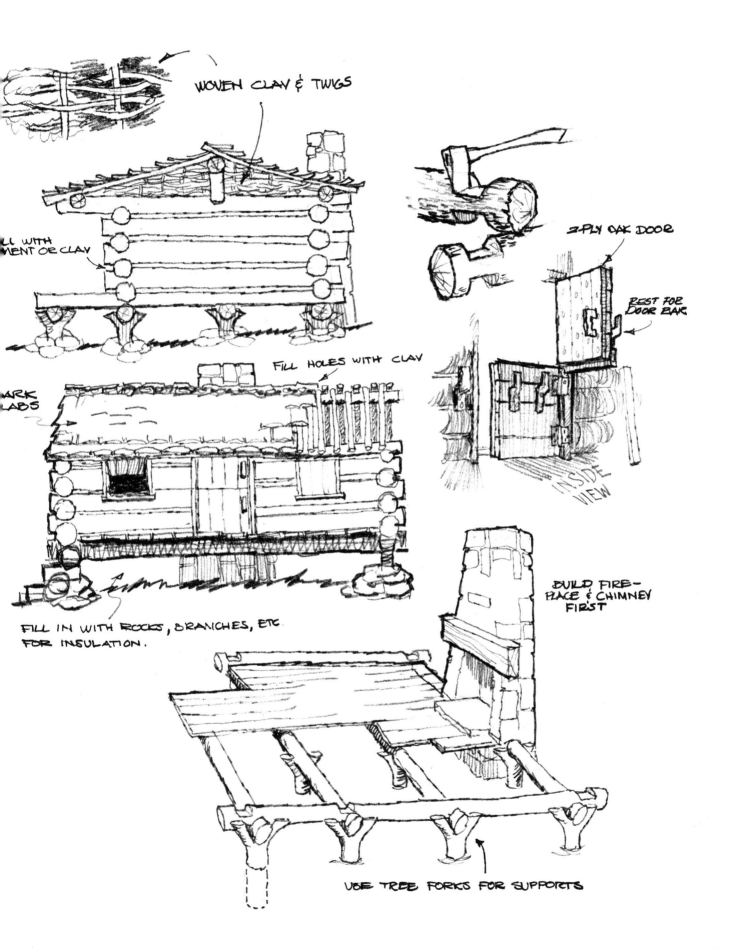

WOVEN CLAY & TWIGS

LL WITH
MENT OR CLAY

ARK
LABS

FILL HOLES WITH CLAY

FILL IN WITH ROCKS, BRANCHES, ETC.
FOR INSULATION.

2-PLY OAK DOOR

REST FOR
DOOR BAR

INSIDE VIEW

BUILD FIRE-
PLACE & CHIMNEY
FIRST

USE TREE FORKS FOR SUPPORTS

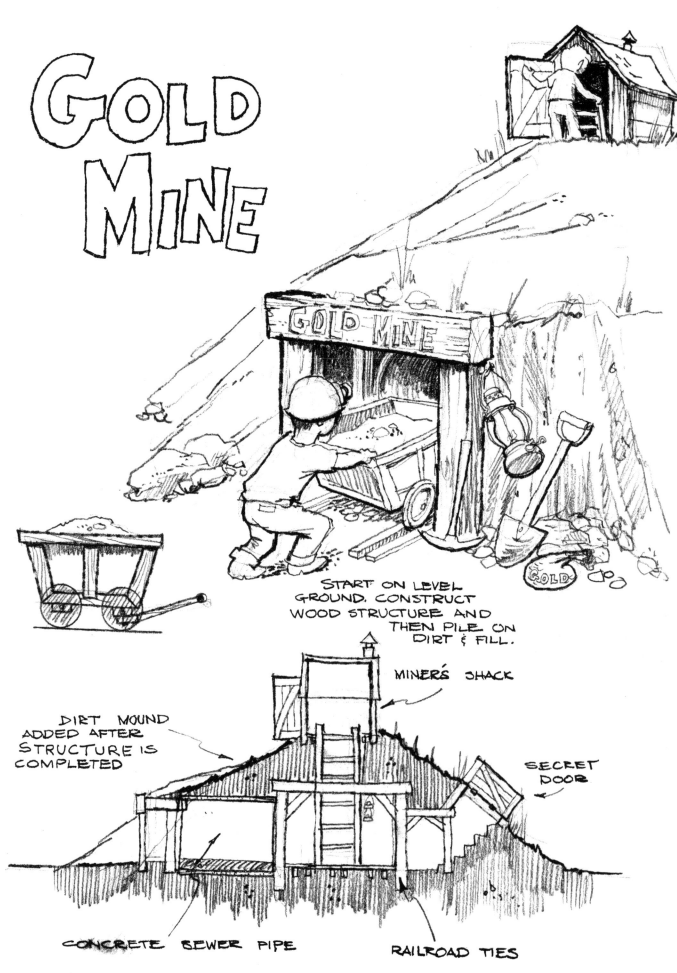

GOLD MINE

START ON LEVEL GROUND. CONSTRUCT WOOD STRUCTURE AND THEN PILE ON DIRT & FILL.

DIRT MOUND ADDED AFTER STRUCTURE IS COMPLETED

MINER'S SHACK

SECRET DOOR

CONCRETE SEWER PIPE

RAILROAD TIES

Jungle Railing

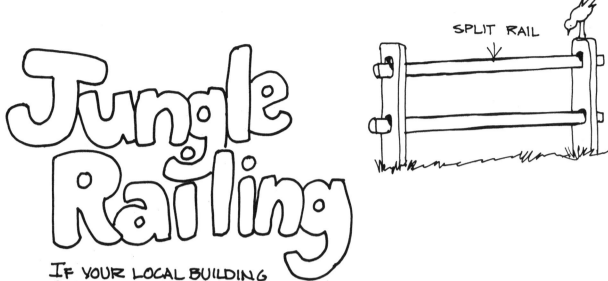

SPLIT RAIL

IF YOUR LOCAL BUILDING SUPPLIER SELLS SPLIT RAILS FOR FENCING YOU ARE IN LUCK BECAUSE THEY CAN BE USED TO MAKE "JURASIC PARK" JUNGLE LOOKING RAILING FOR YOUR TREEHOUSE

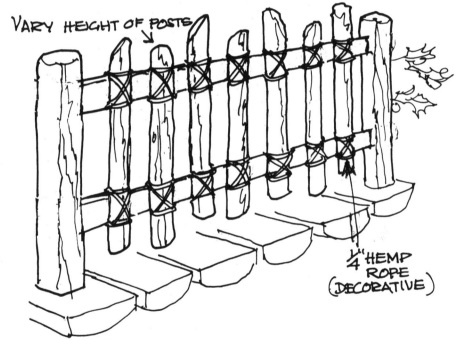

VARY HEIGHT OF POSTS

¼" HEMP ROPE (DECORATIVE)

CUT THE RAILS INTO DIFFERENT LENGTHS AND SCREW THEM (FLAT SIDE TO FLAT SIDE) TO THE TWO HORIZONTAL RAILS. TO MAKE THE RAILING MORE DECORATIVE LASH EACH JOINT WITH ¼" HEMP ROPE.

CUT THE TOP AND BOTTOM OF THE POSTS (BALUSTERS) AT CRAZY ANGLES AND SMOOTH THEM WITH SANDPAPER

CUT HOLES (MORTICES) IN THE CORNER POSTS AND INSERT THE TWO HORIZONTAL RAILS.

SHOE HOUSE

CUT-AWAY-
VIEW

SHOE
HOUSE

3" LAYER SCRATCH
COAT (PLASTER &
SAND.)

2x4 STUDS

2x3 FRAME

WIRE SCREEN

HANSEL AND GRETEL HOUSE

THE HANSEL & GRETEL HOUSE, MADE OF $\frac{1}{2}$" PLYWOOD, MAY TAKE AS LITTLE AS THREE OR FOUR EVENINGS TO MAKE. WE RECOMMEND THAT YOU USE A GOOD, HEAVY-DUTY, ELECTRIC SABER SAW - A GOOD INVESTMENT IN ANY CASE FOR ALL YOUR CUTS. SHINGLES ARE MADE FROM $\frac{1}{4}$" PLYWOOD NAILED OVER ANOTHER $\frac{1}{4}$" SHEET THAT HAS BEEN NAILED TO THE CONTOUR OF ROOF. USE YOUR IMAGINATION FOR THE CANDY DECORATION. IF THE HOUSE IS TO BE KEPT INDOORS YOU CAN USE REAL CANDY AS WE DID. SOME OTHER SUGGESTIONS CAN BE FOUND ON THE FOLLOWING PAGE.

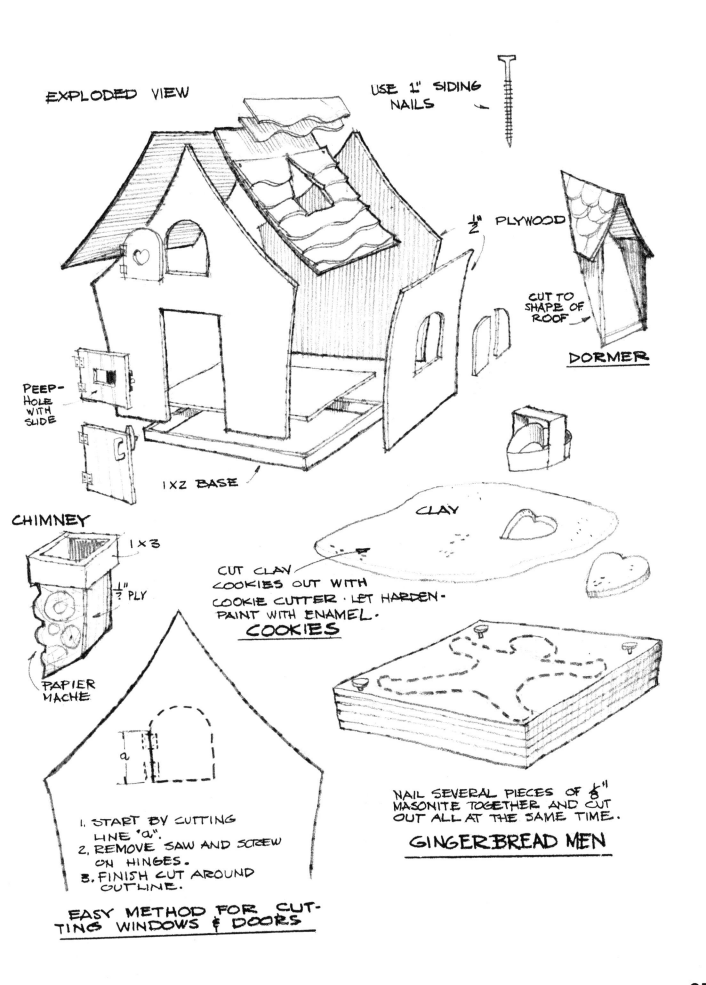

EXPLODED VIEW

USE 1" SIDING NAILS

$\frac{1}{2}$" PLYWOOD

CUT TO SHAPE OF ROOF

DORMER

PEEP- HOLE WITH SLIDE

1 X 2 BASE

CHIMNEY

1 X 3

$\frac{1}{2}$" PLY

PAPIER MACHE

CLAY

CUT CLAY COOKIES OUT WITH COOKIE CUTTER · LET HARDEN · PAINT WITH ENAMEL.
COOKIES

1. START BY CUTTING LINE "a".
2. REMOVE SAW AND SCREW ON HINGES.
3. FINISH CUT AROUND OUTLINE.

EASY METHOD FOR CUTTING WINDOWS & DOORS

NAIL SEVERAL PIECES OF $\frac{1}{8}$" MASONITE TOGETHER AND CUT OUT ALL AT THE SAME TIME.

GINGERBREAD MEN

CLUB HOUSE

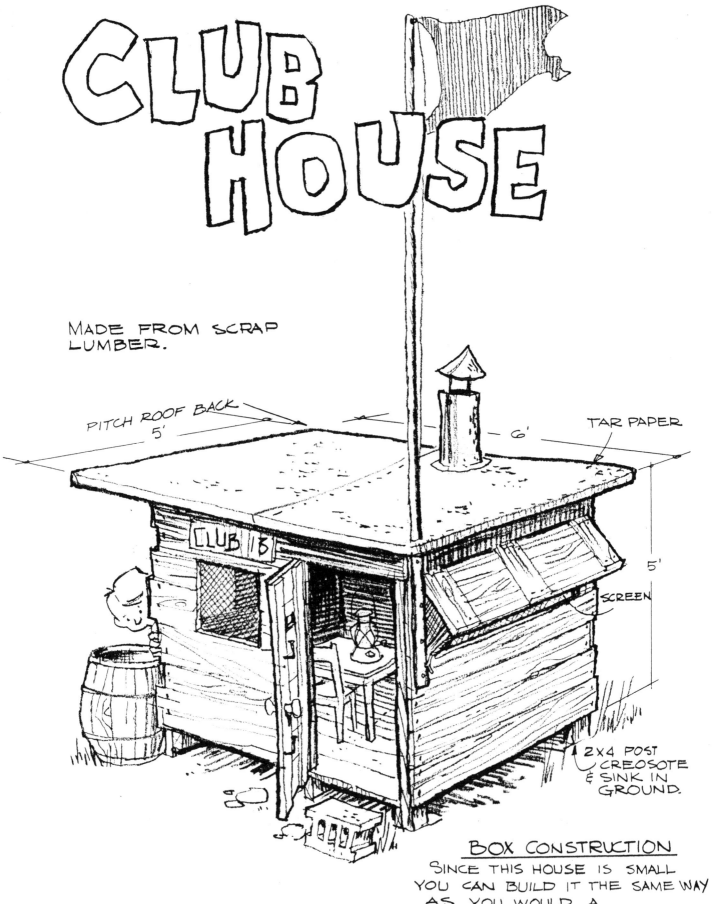

MADE FROM SCRAP LUMBER.

PITCH ROOF BACK 5'

TAR PAPER

6'

5'

SCREEN

CLUB 13

2X4 POST CREOSOTE & SINK IN GROUND.

BOX CONSTRUCTION
SINCE THIS HOUSE IS SMALL YOU CAN BUILD IT THE SAME WAY AS YOU WOULD A BOX. LET THE WALLS ACT AS STRUCTURAL MEMBERS AND USE A MINIMUM OF FRAMING.

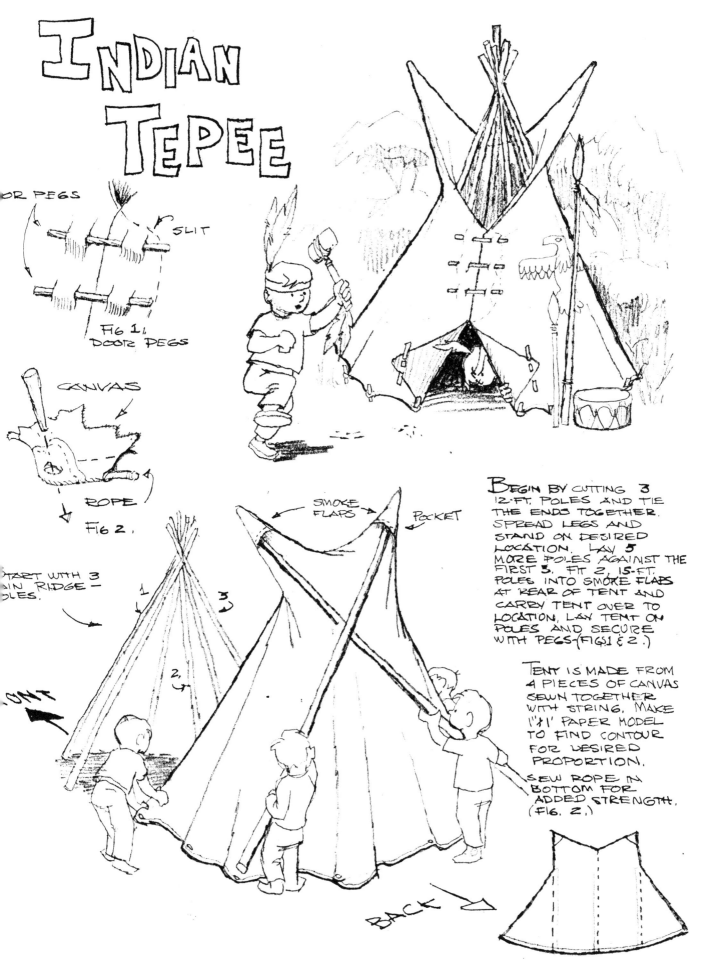

INDIAN TEPEE

OR PEGS

SLIT

FIG 1.
DOOR PEGS

CANVAS

ROPE

FIG 2.

START WITH 3 MAIN RIDGE-POLES.

FRONT

SMOKE FLAPS

POCKET

1

3

2

BACK

BEGIN BY CUTTING 3 12-FT. POLES AND TIE THE ENDS TOGETHER. SPREAD LEGS AND STAND ON DESIRED LOCATION. LAY 5 MORE POLES AGAINST THE FIRST 3. FIT 2, 15-FT. POLES INTO SMOKE FLAPS AT REAR OF TENT AND CARRY TENT OVER TO LOCATION. LAY TENT ON POLES AND SECURE WITH PEGS-(FIGS 1 & 2.)

TENT IS MADE FROM 4 PIECES OF CANVAS SEWN TOGETHER WITH STRING. MAKE 1"=1' PAPER MODEL TO FIND CONTOUR FOR DESIRED PROPORTION.

SEW ROPE IN BOTTOM FOR ADDED STRENGTH. (FIG. 2.)

Jungle House

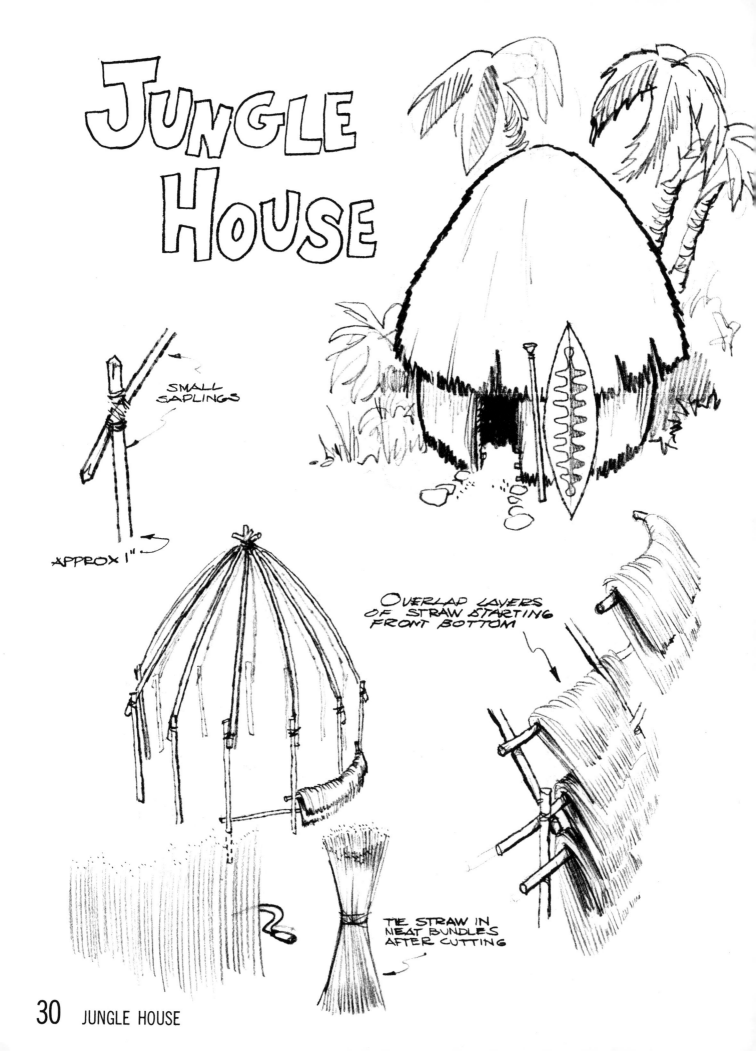

SMALL SAPLINGS

APPROX 1"

OVERLAP LAYERS OF STRAW STARTING FRONT BOTTOM

TIE STRAW IN NEAT BUNDLES AFTER CUTTING

WATER FUN

WATER FUN

WATER is the most important and probably one of the most fascinating elements of nature. In fact, down through history man has been constantly trying new ways to use water for his own benefit. In this section are only a few of the possible ways in which water can be used for having fun. It is up to you to discover more interesting projects; your imagination is your only limit. Consider for example these possibilities for water projects: underwater exploration; water harnessed as power; water used to move objects; floating objects on water, or projects on ice. You be the inventor!

Maybe some of the ideas on the following pages will stimulate your imagination. Remember, whatever you build must be safe, and in some cases it might be wise to have an adult supervise these water activities.

BOUNCING BUOY

THE BOUNCING BUOY IS
SAFE, AND EASY TO MAKE.
IT CAN BE MADE WITH AN
OLD INNER TUBE, 2 BROOM-
STICKS, 2 BOARDS & SOME
ROPE. USE WHATEVER YOU
CAN FIND FOR THE COUNTER-
BALANCING WEIGHT.

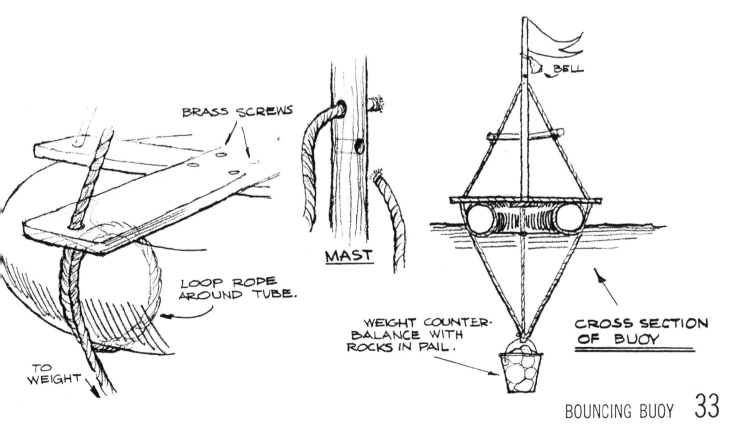

BRASS SCREWS

LOOP ROPE
AROUND TUBE.

TO
WEIGHT

MAST

BELL

WEIGHT COUNTER-
BALANCE WITH
ROCKS IN PAIL.

CROSS SECTION
OF BUOY

JOUSTING LOG

THE JOUSTING LOG IS A
SAFE SPORT FOR ANY WATER-
FRONT.

THE OBJECT IS TO BALANCE
YOURSELF ON THE LOG AND
PUSH YOUR OPPONENT OFF
WITHOUT FALLING OFF YOURSELF.

BROOM STICK STAVES.
WRAP COTTON AND CLOTH
STRIPS AROUND ENDS OR
USE BOXING GLOVES.

STRIP BARK
OFF LOG AND
SAND OFF ROUGH
SURFACES.

FLOAT LOG WITH LARGE
INNER TUBE OR OLD OIL
BARREL.

TARZAN SWING

FIND A TREE THAT HAS A STRONG LIMB STRETCHING OUT OVER THE WATER. THROW A WEIGHTED ROPE, WITH A LOOP TIED INTO THE END OF THE ROPE, OVER THE BRANCH. PLACE THE OTHER END OF THE THROUGH THE LOOP AND PULL THE ROPE UP TIGHT ONTO THE BRANCH. TIE SOME KNOTS INTO THE LOOSE END OF THE ROPE TO HAVE SOMETHING TO HOLD ONTO. IF NECESSARY BUILD AN ELEVATED LAUNCHING PLATFORM SET BACK FROM THE SHORELINE.

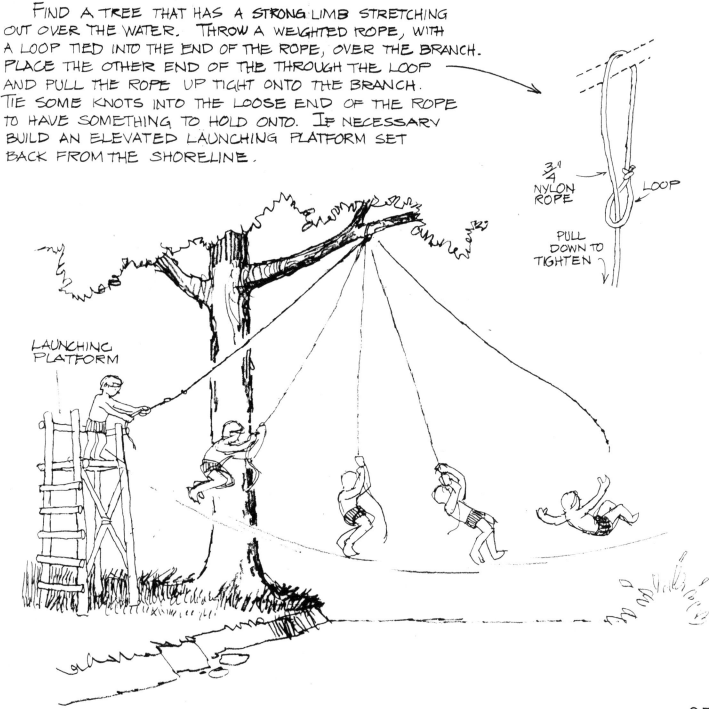

$\frac{3}{4}$" NYLON ROPE

LOOP

PULL DOWN TO TIGHTEN

LAUNCHING PLATFORM

BALLOON RAFT

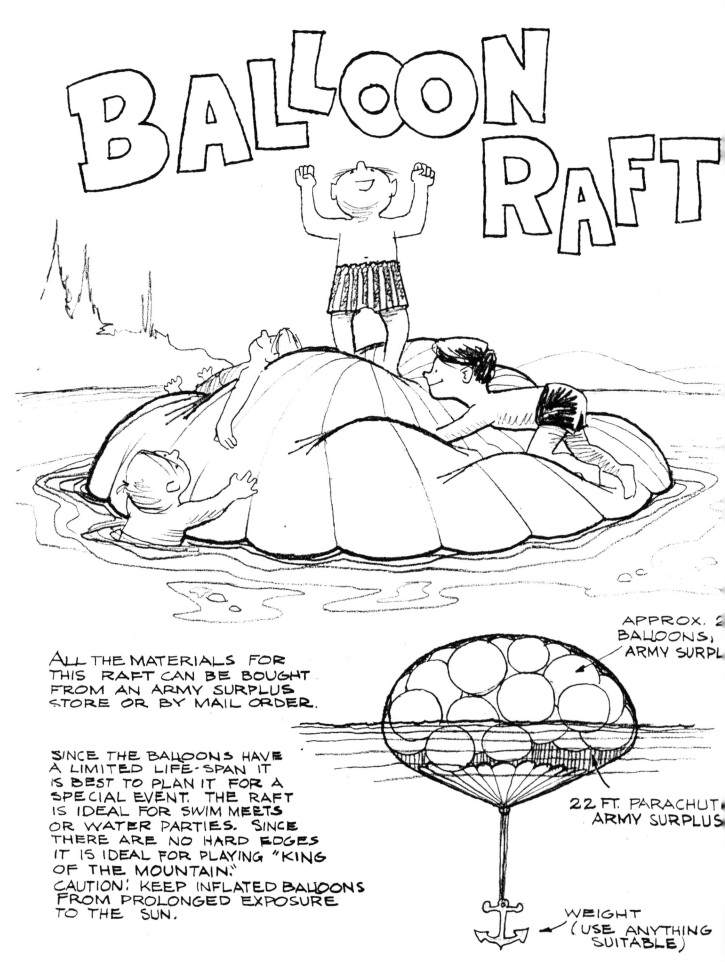

ALL THE MATERIALS FOR THIS RAFT CAN BE BOUGHT FROM AN ARMY SURPLUS STORE OR BY MAIL ORDER.

SINCE THE BALLOONS HAVE A LIMITED LIFE-SPAN IT IS BEST TO PLAN IT FOR A SPECIAL EVENT. THE RAFT IS IDEAL FOR SWIM MEETS OR WATER PARTIES. SINCE THERE ARE NO HARD EDGES IT IS IDEAL FOR PLAYING "KING OF THE MOUNTAIN." CAUTION: KEEP INFLATED BALLOONS FROM PROLONGED EXPOSURE TO THE SUN.

APPROX. 2 BALLOONS, ARMY SURPL

22 FT. PARACHUT ARMY SURPLUS

WEIGHT (USE ANYTHING SUITABLE)

LOG RAFT

CUT FOUR PINE LOGS 10" TO 12" IN DIAMETER AND LASH THEM TOGETHER WITH HEMP ROPE. DRIVE TWO OAK PEGS INTO THE TWO CENTER LOGS IN THE STERN AND USE THESE TO REST THE OAR IN. USE THE OAR AS A RUDDER WHEN THE SAIL IS UP OR USE IT TO "SKULL" WITH IF THE SAIL IS DOWN. USE A BLANKET OR SHEET AS A SAIL.

WHALE RAFT

A <u>WHALE RAFT</u> CAN BE A LOT OF FUN FOR CHILDREN AND AT THE SAME TIME SERVE AS A SAFETY FEATURE AT SWIMMING AREAS. THE MOUTH OF THE WHALE OPENS AND CLOSES BY PULLING A ROPE ATTACHED TO THE FRONT UP AND RUNNING THROUGH A PULLEY AT THE TOP.

MAKE RAFT AS SHOWN ON FOLLOWING PAGE OR WITH STEEL BARRELS.

CLOTH COVERING CAN BE EITHER CANVAS OR OLD BED SHEETS.

TEETH MADE FROM PIECES OF SCRAP FOAM RUBBER OR CUT OUT FROM A LONG STRIP OF CLOTH

MOUTH MOVES UP AND DOWN

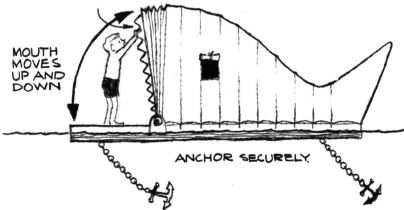

ANCHOR SECURELY.

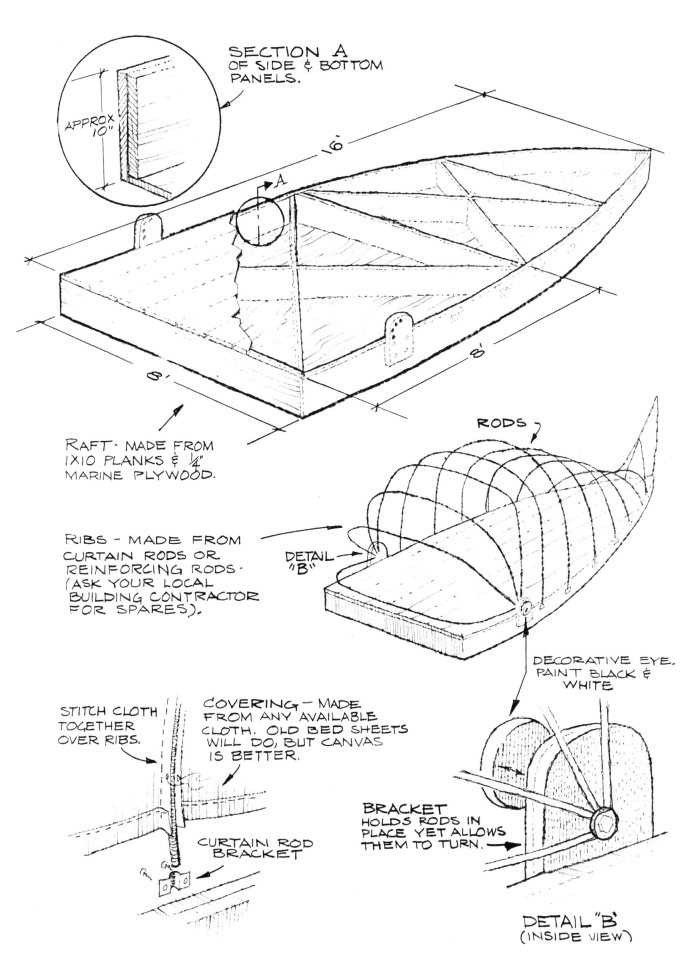

SECTION A
OF SIDE & BOTTOM
PANELS.

APPROX
10"

6'

8'

8'

A

RAFT· MADE FROM
1X10 PLANKS & ¼"
MARINE PLYWOOD.

RIBS - MADE FROM
CURTAIN RODS OR
REINFORCING RODS·
(ASK YOUR LOCAL
BUILDING CONTRACTOR
FOR SPARES).

RODS

DETAIL
"B"

DECORATIVE EYE.
PAINT BLACK &
WHITE

STITCH CLOTH
TOGETHER
OVER RIBS.

COVERING — MADE
FROM ANY AVAILABLE
CLOTH. OLD BED SHEETS
WILL DO, BUT CANVAS
IS BETTER.

CURTAIN ROD
BRACKET

BRACKET
HOLDS RODS IN
PLACE YET ALLOWS
THEM TO TURN.

DETAIL "B"
(INSIDE VIEW)

WHALE RAFT (DETAILS)   39

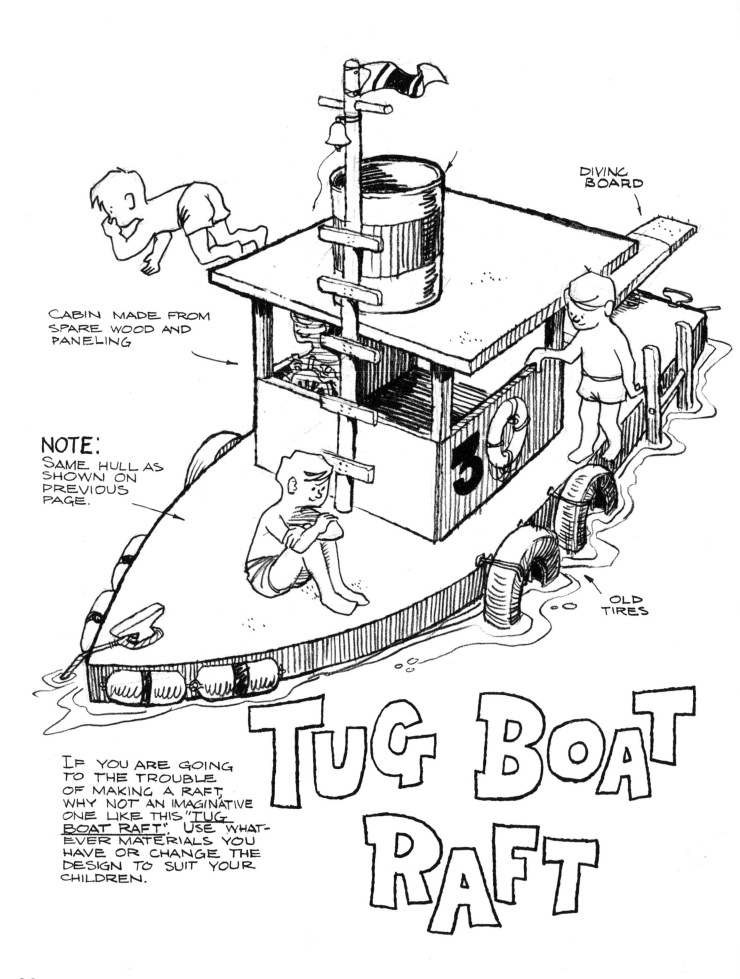

DIVING BOARD

CABIN MADE FROM SPARE WOOD AND PANELING

NOTE: SAME HULL AS SHOWN ON PREVIOUS PAGE.

OLD TIRES

TUG BOAT RAFT

IF YOU ARE GOING TO THE TROUBLE OF MAKING A RAFT, WHY NOT AN IMAGINATIVE ONE LIKE THIS "TUG BOAT RAFT". USE WHATEVER MATERIALS YOU HAVE OR CHANGE THE DESIGN TO SUIT YOUR CHILDREN.

MODEL SAIL BOAT

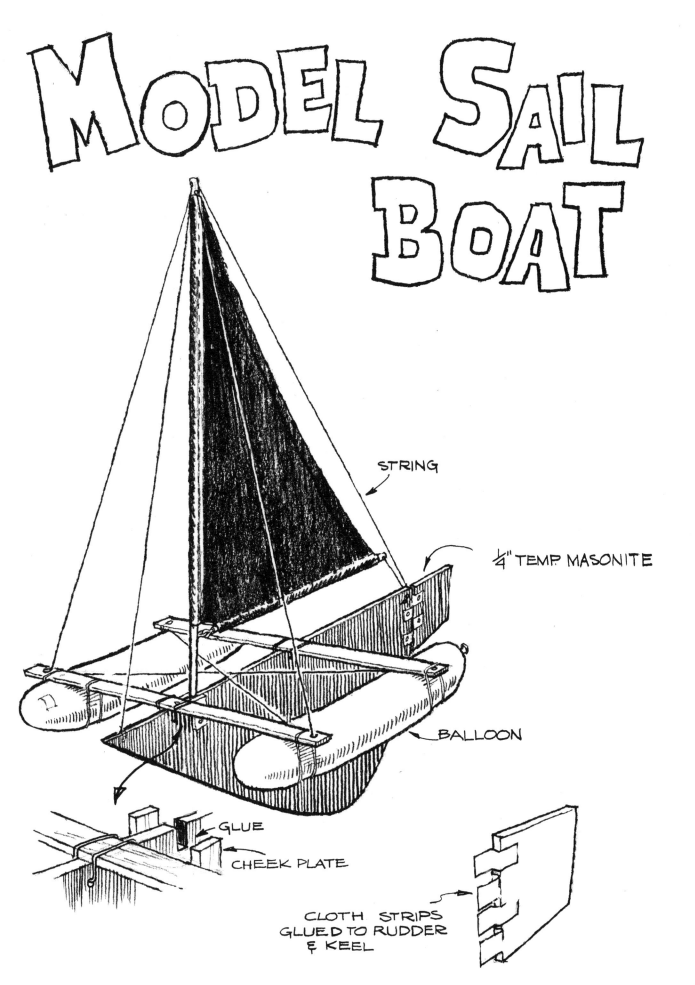

STRING

¼" TEMP. MASONITE

BALLOON

GLUE

CHEEK PLATE

CLOTH STRIPS
GLUED TO RUDDER
& KEEL

STEAM BOAT

THIS MODEL STEAM BOAT CAN BE MADE CHEAPLY AND EASILY WITH A FEW SMALL PIECES OF WOOD, WIRE, SCRAP METAL, AN OLD CAN, TUBING, AND A CAN OF STERNO.
THE BOAT IS PROPELLED BY STEAM MADE BY HEATING WATER IN A CAN AND FORCING THE STEAM THROUGH A TUBE OUT AT THE BACK.

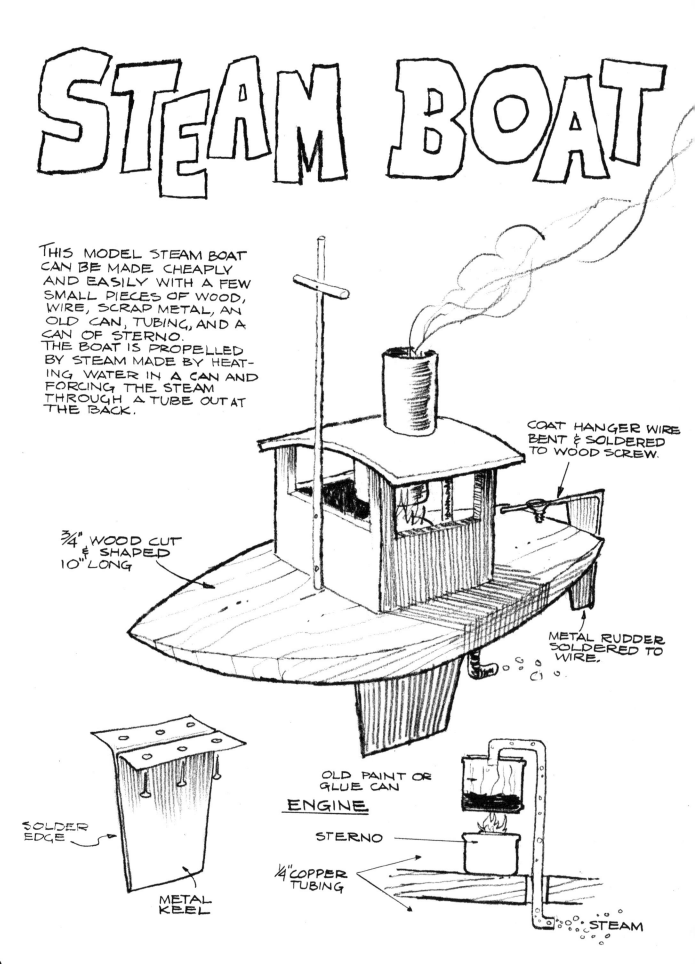

COAT HANGER WIRE BENT & SOLDERED TO WOOD SCREW.

¾" WOOD CUT & SHAPED 10" LONG

METAL RUDDER SOLDERED TO WIRE.

SOLDER EDGE

METAL KEEL

OLD PAINT OR GLUE CAN

ENGINE

STERNO

¼" COPPER TUBING

STEAM

4 FT. SAIL-BOAT

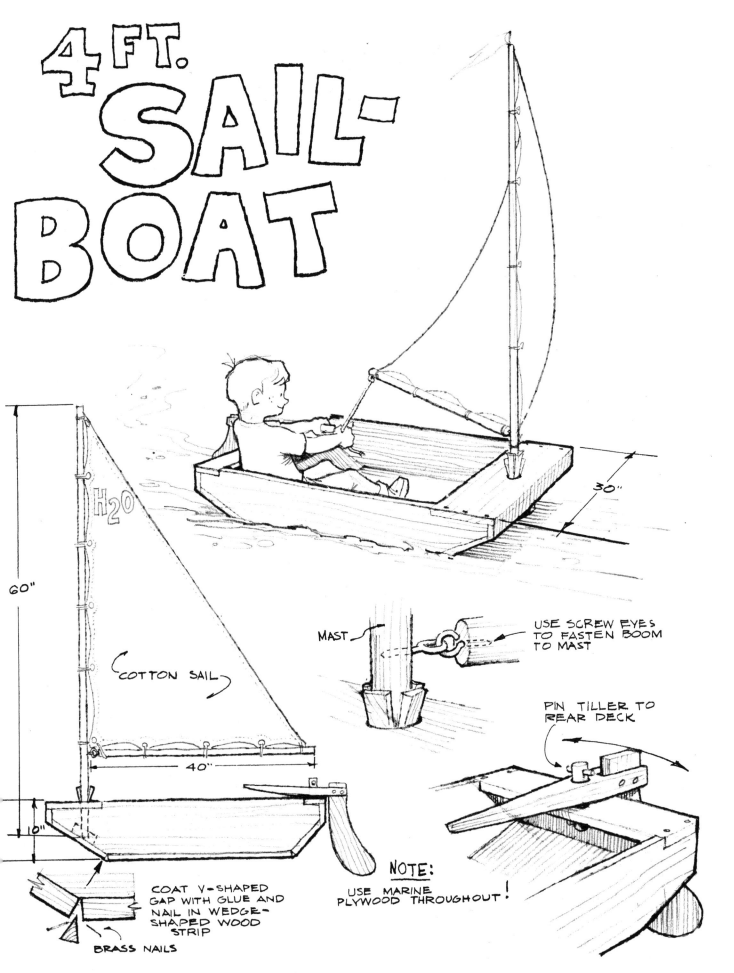

60"

H₂O

COTTON SAIL

40"

10"

COAT V-SHAPED GAP WITH GLUE AND NAIL IN WEDGE-SHAPED WOOD STRIP

BRASS NAILS

30"

MAST

USE SCREW EYES TO FASTEN BOOM TO MAST

PIN TILLER TO REAR DECK

NOTE:
USE MARINE PLYWOOD THROUGHOUT!

6ft.

SAIL-
BOAT

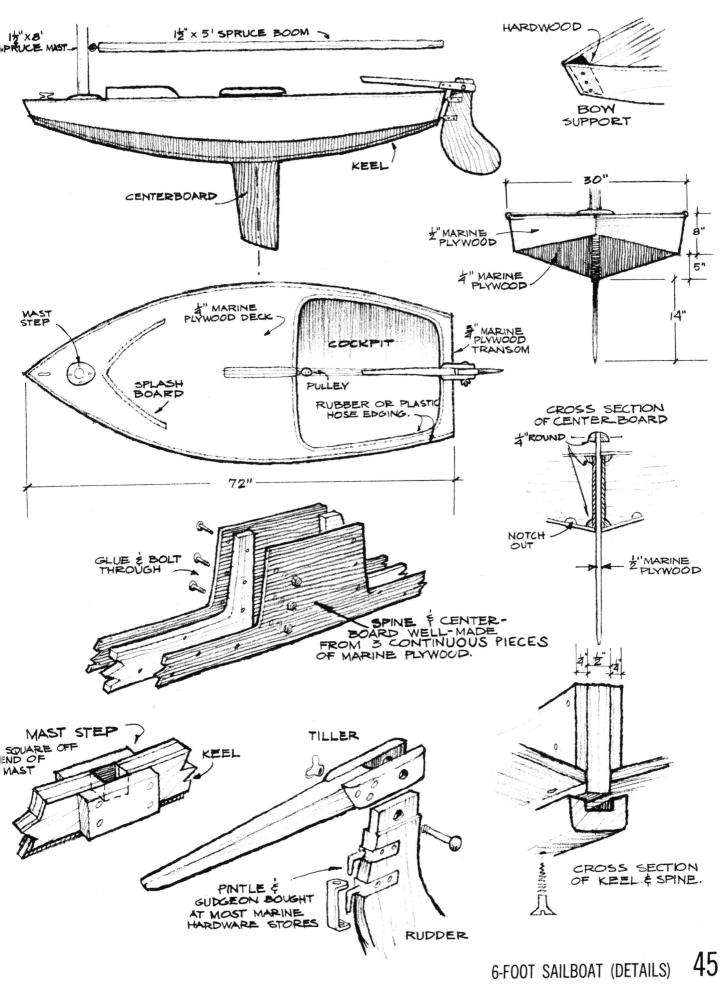

1½" x 8' SPRUCE MAST

1½" x 5' SPRUCE BOOM

HARDWOOD

BOW SUPPORT

KEEL

CENTERBOARD

30"

½" MARINE PLYWOOD

¼" MARINE PLYWOOD

8"

5"

14"

MAST STEP

¼" MARINE PLYWOOD DECK

COCKPIT

¾" MARINE PLYWOOD TRANSOM

SPLASH BOARD

PULLEY

RUBBER OR PLASTIC HOSE EDGING.

72"

CROSS SECTION OF CENTER BOARD

¼" ROUND

NOTCH OUT

½" MARINE PLYWOOD

GLUE & BOLT THROUGH

SPINE & CENTER-BOARD WELL MADE FROM 3 CONTINUOUS PIECES OF MARINE PLYWOOD.

¼" ½" ¼"

MAST STEP

SQUARE OFF END OF MAST

KEEL

TILLER

PINTLE & GUDGEON BOUGHT AT MOST MARINE HARDWARE STORES

RUDDER

CROSS SECTION OF KEEL & SPINE.

6-FOOT SAILBOAT (DETAILS) 45

ROW-BOAT

STEP 2. SOAK SIDE BOARDS IN WATER FOR SEVERAL DAYS AND BEND AROUND SPACER.

STEP 3. FASTEN SIDE BOARDS SECURELY TO TRANSOM AND SAW OFF EXCESS.

STEP 1. FASTEN BOW TOGETHER

STEP 4. GLUE & SCREW FLOOR PANEL TO SIDE BOARDS & TRANSOM AND TRIM OFF.

SPACER

2½'

6 FT.

3'

12"

HARDWOOD

SIDE PANEL

GLUE & SCREW

SECTION OF BOW ASSEMBLY

SUGGESTIONS

THE HOUSE FOR THE HOUSEBOAT CAN BE MADE SEVERAL WAYS:

ONE WAY IS TO MAKE IT OUT OF 3/4" PLYWOOD WITH A MINIMUM AMOUNT OF FRAMING. (EASIEST)

ANOTHER WAY IS TO ROUGH-FRAME THE HOUSE WITH 2x4's AND COVER WITH 1/8" MASONITE (TEMPERED) OR 1/4" PLYWOOD AND PAINT. (CHEAPEST)

A THIRD WAY IS TO USE 2x2 FRAMING AND CLAP BOARD SIDING WITH T&G ROOFING COVERED WITH SHINGLES. (BEST BUT EXPENSIVE)

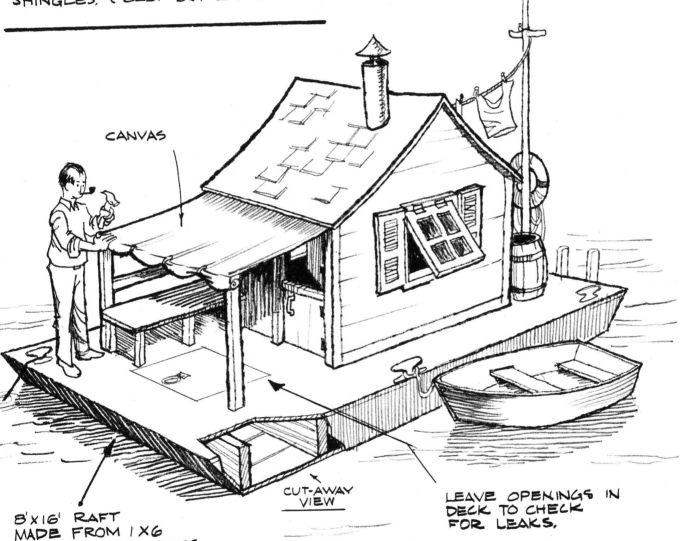

CANVAS

CUT-AWAY VIEW

8'x16' RAFT MADE FROM 1x6 T&G & 1x12 CROSS MEMBERS. FIBERGLAS JOINTS AND PAINT BOTTOM WITH POLYESTER RESIN.

LEAVE OPENINGS IN DECK TO CHECK FOR LEAKS.

INDOOR PROJECTS

DOLL HOUSE

WALLS & ROOF MADE OF 1/8" MASONITE

DECORATE WITH STRIPS OF BALSA WOOD

YELLOW BARN

CLAY

SECTION SWINGS OUT

1/4" PLYWOOD BASE

BALSA WOOD

PAPER SHINGLES

PIÑATA PARTY

THE PIÑATA IS A MEXICAN TRADITIC ORIGINALLY USED DURING THE NINE DAYS OF CHRISTMAS. IN PRESENT-DAY MEXICO THEY ARE USED AT BIRTHDAY PARTIES AND GENERALLY FILLED WITH FRUIT AND CANDY AND SOMETIMES TOYS. THE PIÑATA IS HUNG FROM THE CEILING AND EACH CHILD IS GIVEN A CHANCE TO BREAK IT WITH A STICK. WHEN IT FINALLY DOES BREAK THERE IS A MAD SCRAMBLE FOR THE GOODIES INSIDE.

How To Make A Piñata

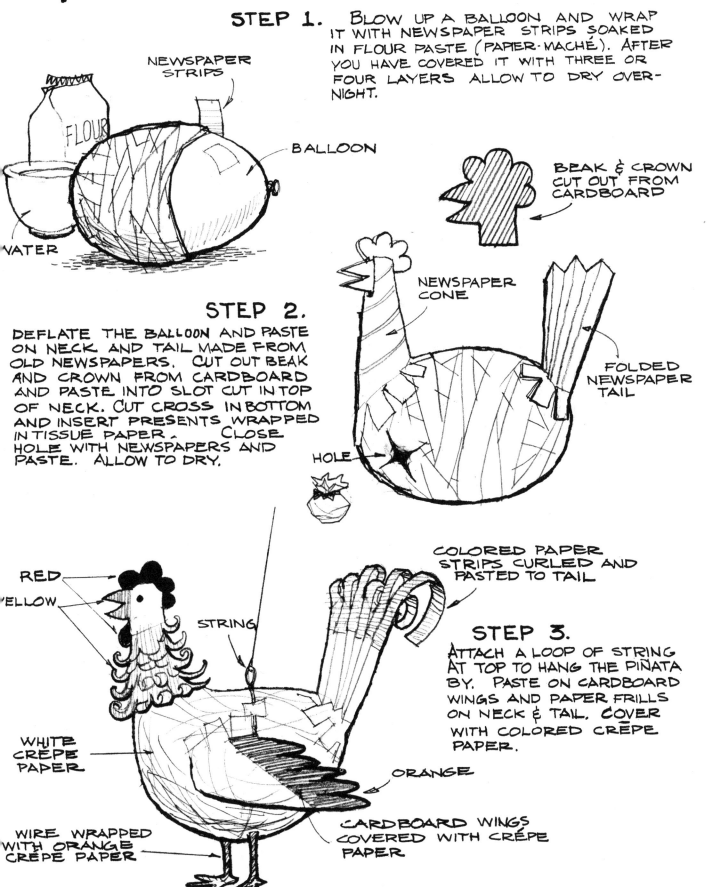

STEP 1. Blow up a balloon and wrap it with newspaper strips soaked in flour paste (papier-maché). After you have covered it with three or four layers allow to dry overnight.

NEWSPAPER STRIPS

FLOUR

WATER

BALLOON

BEAK & CROWN CUT OUT FROM CARDBOARD

STEP 2.

Deflate the balloon and paste on neck and tail made from old newspapers. Cut out beak and crown from cardboard and paste into slot cut in top of neck. Cut cross in bottom and insert presents wrapped in tissue paper. Close hole with newspapers and paste. Allow to dry.

NEWSPAPER CONE

FOLDED NEWSPAPER TAIL

HOLE

COLORED PAPER STRIPS CURLED AND PASTED TO TAIL

STEP 3.

Attach a loop of string at top to hang the piñata by. Paste on cardboard wings and paper frills on neck & tail. Cover with colored crépe paper.

RED

YELLOW

STRING

WHITE CREPE PAPER

ORANGE

CARDBOARD WINGS COVERED WITH CRÉPE PAPER

WIRE WRAPPED WITH ORANGE CRÉPE PAPER

CLAY CASTLE

HINTS ON MAKING CLAY STRUCTURES

USE A GOOD GRADE OF WATER-BASE CLAY. KNEAD THE CLAY ON A PIECE OF PLASTER SO IT IS SOMEWHAT HEAVIER THAN THICK PEANUT-BUTTER. USE THE METHODS SHOWN BELOW FOR BUILDING UP STRONG STRUCTURES. ALLOW SEVERAL DAYS TO DRY. STRUCTURES MAY BE PAINTED WITH ORDINARY ENAMEL PAINT OR THEY MAY BE FIRED IN A KILN IN SECTIONS.

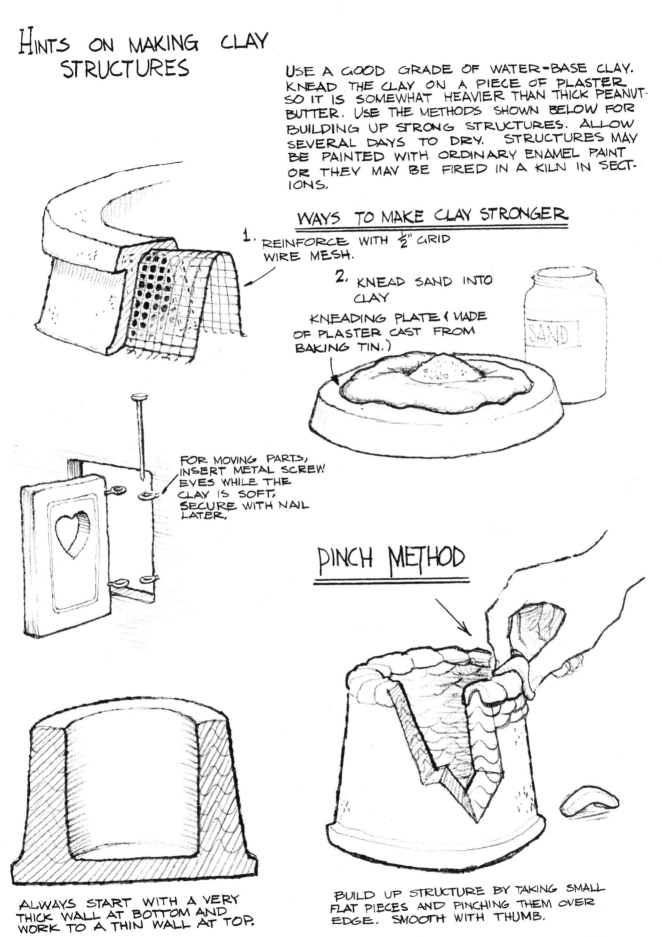

WAYS TO MAKE CLAY STRONGER

1. REINFORCE WITH $\frac{1}{2}$" GRID WIRE MESH.

2. KNEAD SAND INTO CLAY

KNEADING PLATE (MADE OF PLASTER CAST FROM BAKING TIN.)

SAND

FOR MOVING PARTS, INSERT METAL SCREW EYES WHILE THE CLAY IS SOFT, SECURE WITH NAIL LATER.

PINCH METHOD

ALWAYS START WITH A VERY THICK WALL AT BOTTOM AND WORK TO A THIN WALL AT TOP.

BUILD UP STRUCTURE BY TAKING SMALL FLAT PIECES AND PINCHING THEM OVER EDGE. SMOOTH WITH THUMB.

YOU CAN MAKE ANY STRUCTURE YOU WANT IF YOU FOLLOW THESE BASIC PRINCIPLES

WHEELBARROW

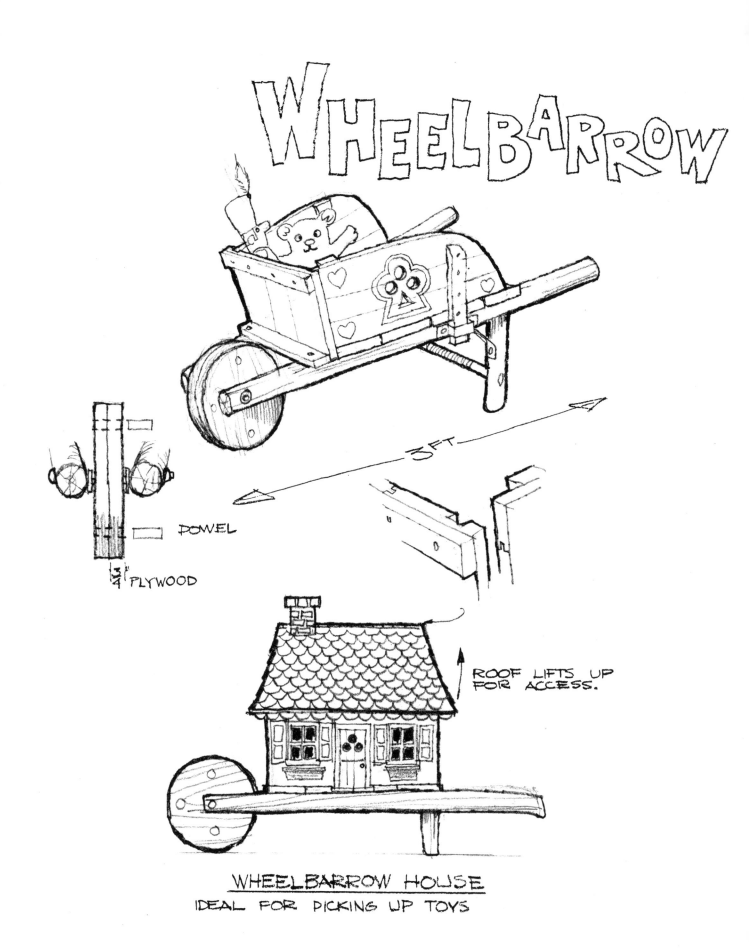

DOWEL

3/4 PLYWOOD

3FT

ROOF LIFTS UP FOR ACCESS.

WHEELBARROW HOUSE
IDEAL FOR PICKING UP TOYS

ROUND HOUSE
Toy Pick-up

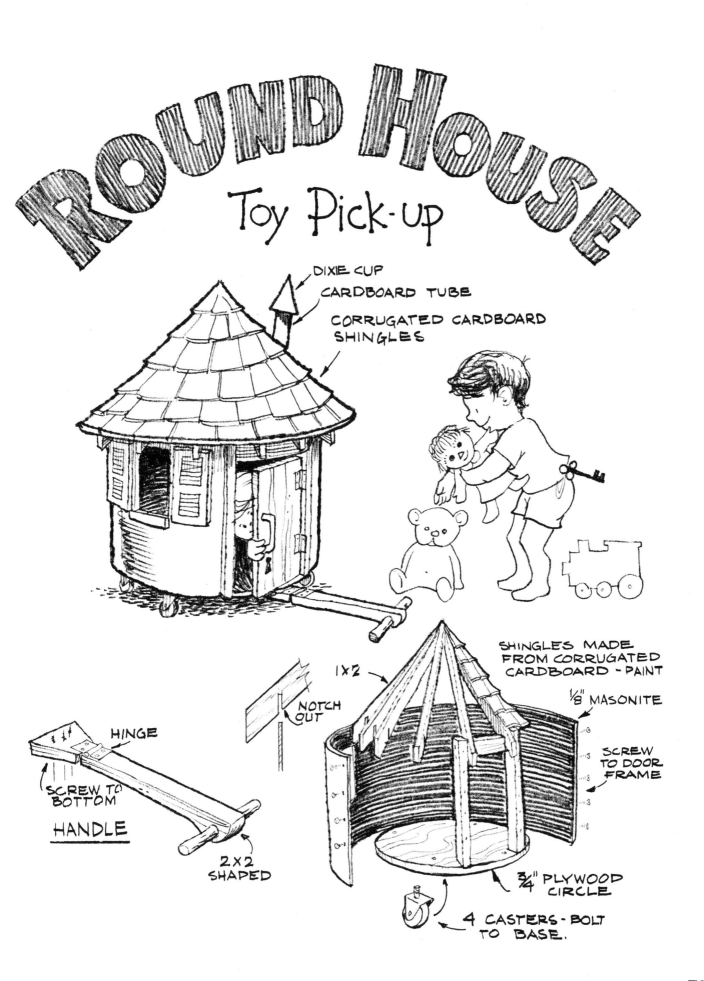

DIXIE CUP

CARDBOARD TUBE

CORRUGATED CARDBOARD SHINGLES

SHINGLES MADE FROM CORRUGATED CARDBOARD - PAINT

1/8" MASONITE

1x2

NOTCH OUT

SCREW TO DOOR FRAME

HINGE

SCREW TO BOTTOM

HANDLE

2X2 SHAPED

3/4" PLYWOOD CIRCLE

4 CASTERS - BOLT TO BASE.

TOY BINS

FROG

SERVE AS STORAGE FOR SMALL TOYS AND MAKE PICKING UP TOYS FUN FOR THE CHILD.

BOLT & WASHER BECOME EYE OF FROG

MADE ENTIRELY FROM $\frac{1}{2}$" PLYWOOD.

USE $\frac{1}{8}$" HARDBOARD SOAK IN HOT WATER FOR 1 HR. BEFORE BENDING.

FISH

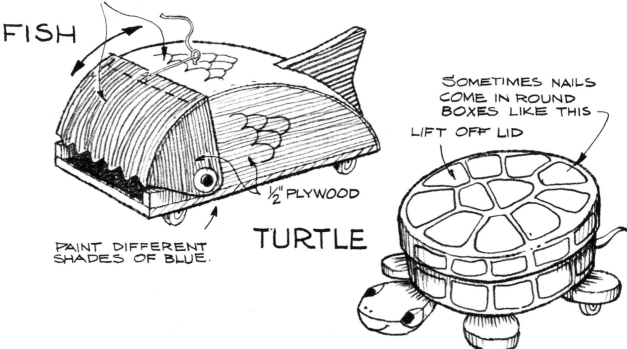

SOMETIMES NAILS COME IN ROUND BOXES LIKE THIS

LIFT OFF LID

$\frac{1}{2}$" PLYWOOD

PAINT DIFFERENT SHADES OF BLUE.

TURTLE

KANGAROO

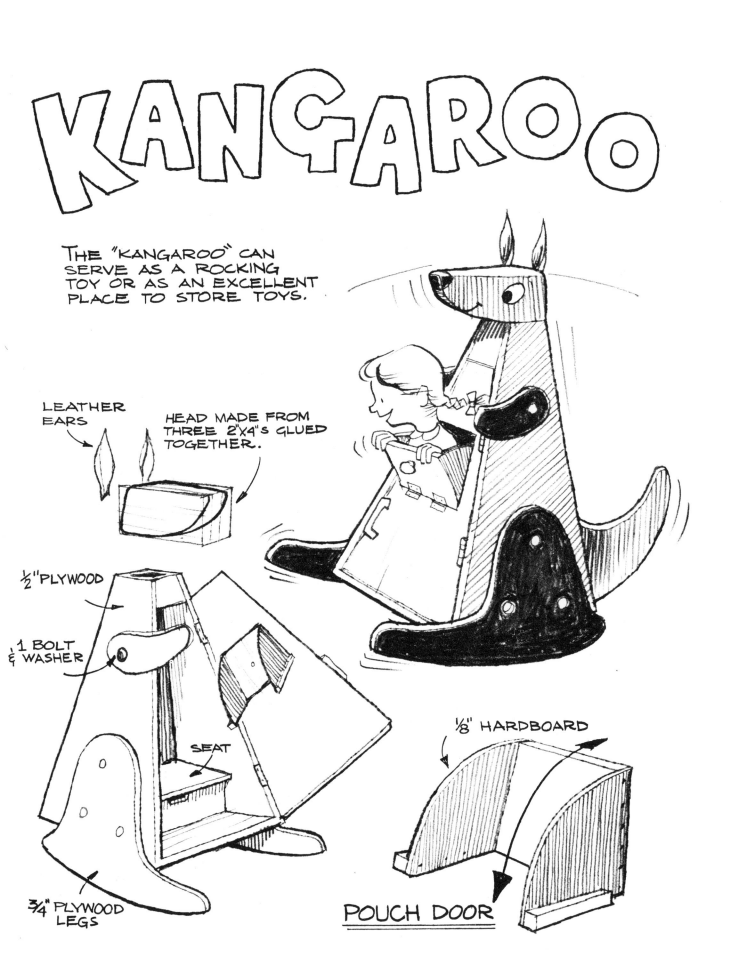

THE "KANGAROO" CAN SERVE AS A ROCKING TOY OR AS AN EXCELLENT PLACE TO STORE TOYS.

LEATHER EARS

HEAD MADE FROM THREE 2"x4"S GLUED TOGETHER.

½" PLYWOOD

1 BOLT & WASHER

SEAT

¾" PLYWOOD LEGS

⅛" HARDBOARD

POUCH DOOR

EASY-TO-
MAKE —

Llama

TOY PICK-UP

MADE FROM OLD 2 X 4's
AND A BOX.

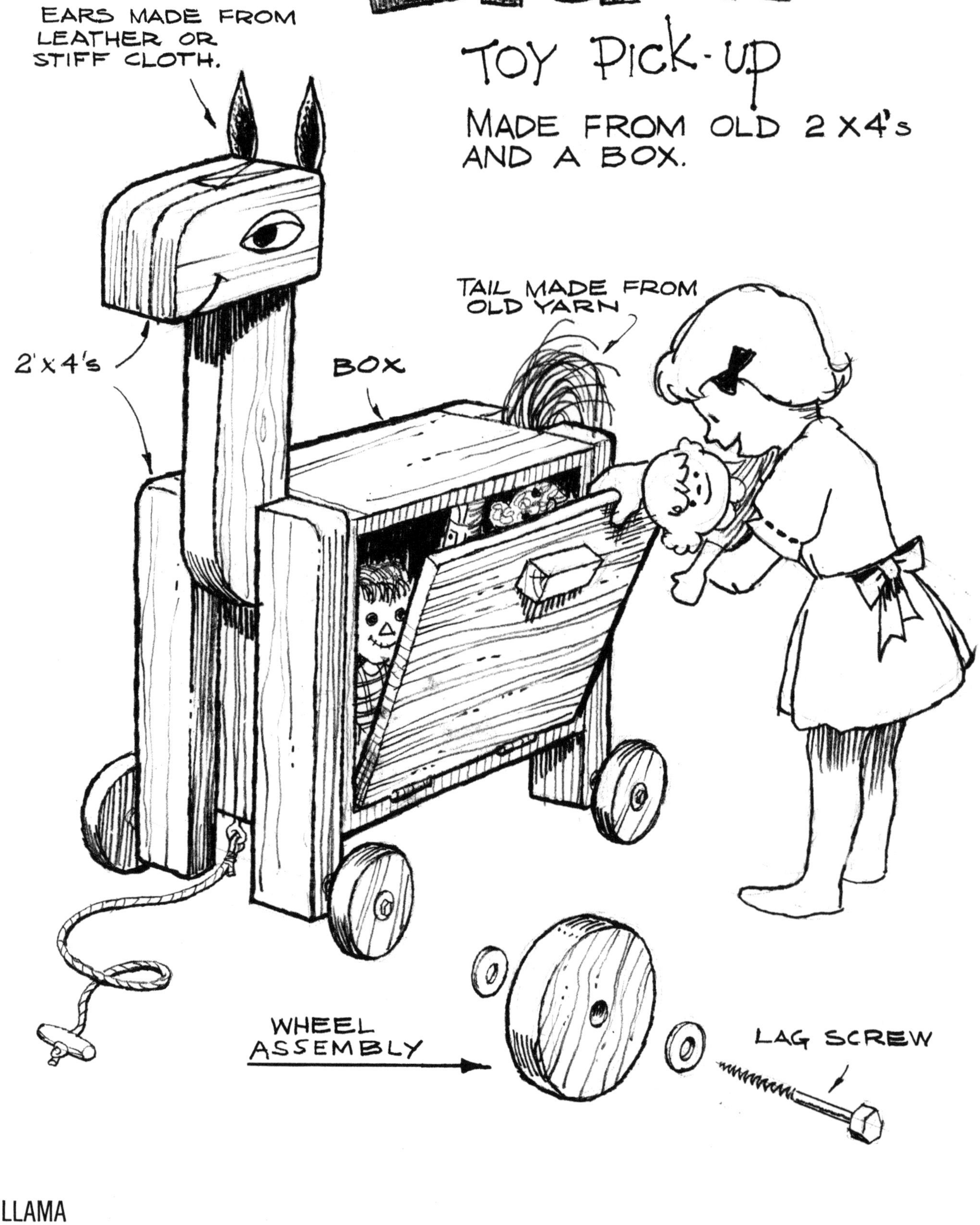

EARS MADE FROM
LEATHER OR
STIFF CLOTH.

2'x4's

BOX

TAIL MADE FROM
OLD YARN

WHEEL
ASSEMBLY

LAG SCREW

3 ROCKING HORSES

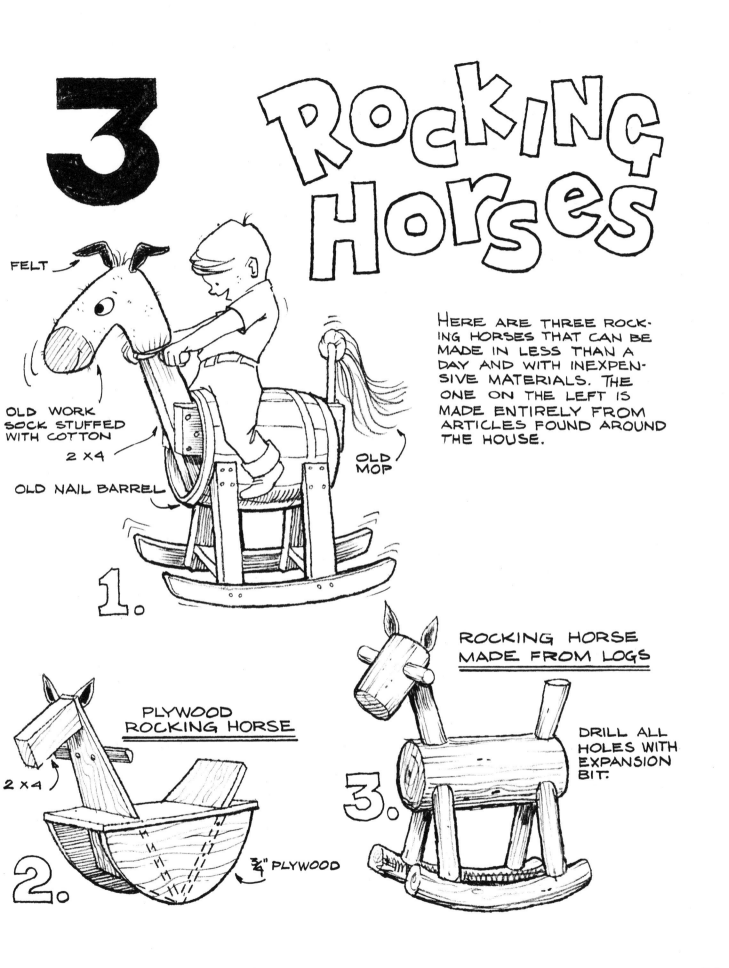

FELT

OLD WORK SOCK STUFFED WITH COTTON

2 x 4

OLD NAIL BARREL

OLD MOP

HERE ARE THREE ROCKING HORSES THAT CAN BE MADE IN LESS THAN A DAY AND WITH INEXPENSIVE MATERIALS. THE ONE ON THE LEFT IS MADE ENTIRELY FROM ARTICLES FOUND AROUND THE HOUSE.

1.

PLYWOOD ROCKING HORSE

2 X 4

¾" PLYWOOD

2.

ROCKING HORSE MADE FROM LOGS

DRILL ALL HOLES WITH EXPANSION BIT.

3.

EASY-TO-MAKE FURNITURE

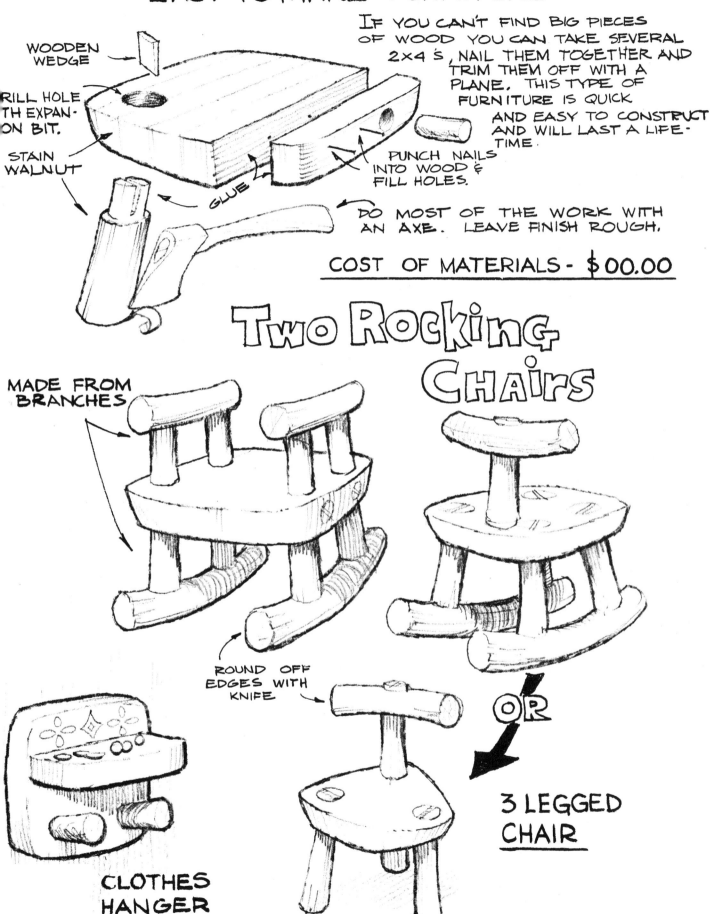

IF YOU CAN'T FIND BIG PIECES OF WOOD YOU CAN TAKE SEVERAL 2×4'S, NAIL THEM TOGETHER AND TRIM THEM OFF WITH A PLANE. THIS TYPE OF FURNITURE IS QUICK AND EASY TO CONSTRUCT AND WILL LAST A LIFE-TIME.

WOODEN WEDGE

RILL HOLE TH EXPAN-ON BIT.

STAIN WALNUT

GLUE

PUNCH NAILS INTO WOOD & FILL HOLES.

DO MOST OF THE WORK WITH AN AXE. LEAVE FINISH ROUGH.

COST OF MATERIALS - $00.00

Two Rocking Chairs

MADE FROM BRANCHES

ROUND OFF EDGES WITH KNIFE

OR

3 LEGGED CHAIR

CLOTHES HANGER

Marble Ladder

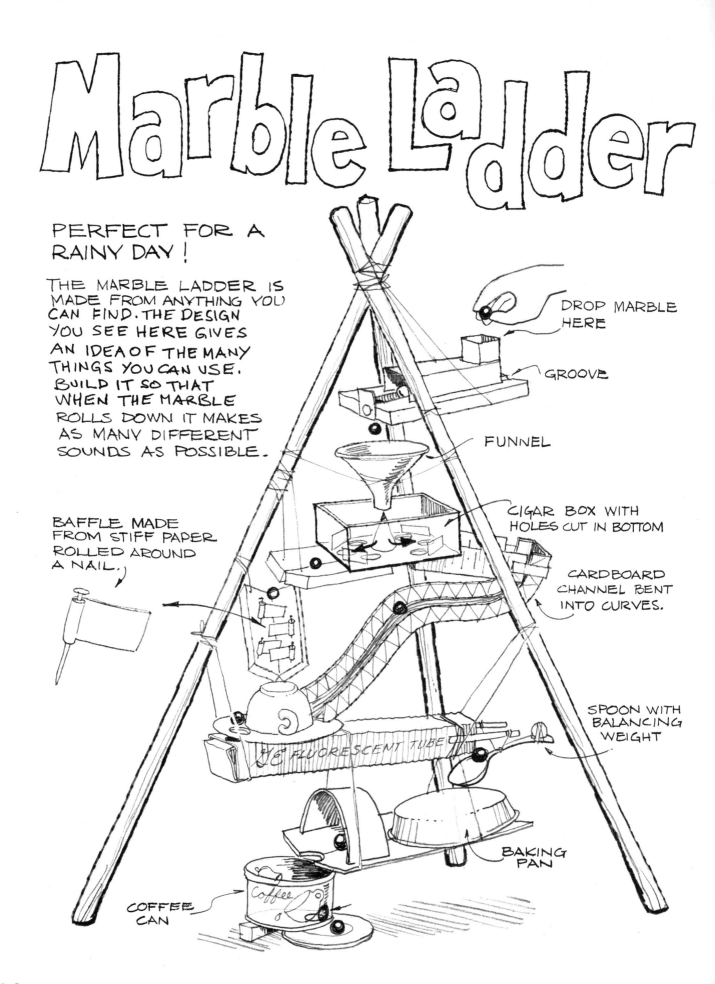

PERFECT FOR A RAINY DAY!

THE MARBLE LADDER IS MADE FROM ANYTHING YOU CAN FIND. THE DESIGN YOU SEE HERE GIVES AN IDEA OF THE MANY THINGS YOU CAN USE. BUILD IT SO THAT WHEN THE MARBLE ROLLS DOWN IT MAKES AS MANY DIFFERENT SOUNDS AS POSSIBLE.

DROP MARBLE HERE

GROOVE

FUNNEL

CIGAR BOX WITH HOLES CUT IN BOTTOM

CARDBOARD CHANNEL BENT INTO CURVES.

BAFFLE MADE FROM STIFF PAPER ROLLED AROUND A NAIL.

SPOON WITH BALANCING WEIGHT

FLUORESCENT TUBE

BAKING PAN

COFFEE CAN

Coffee

OUTDOOR PROJECTS

CROSS BOW

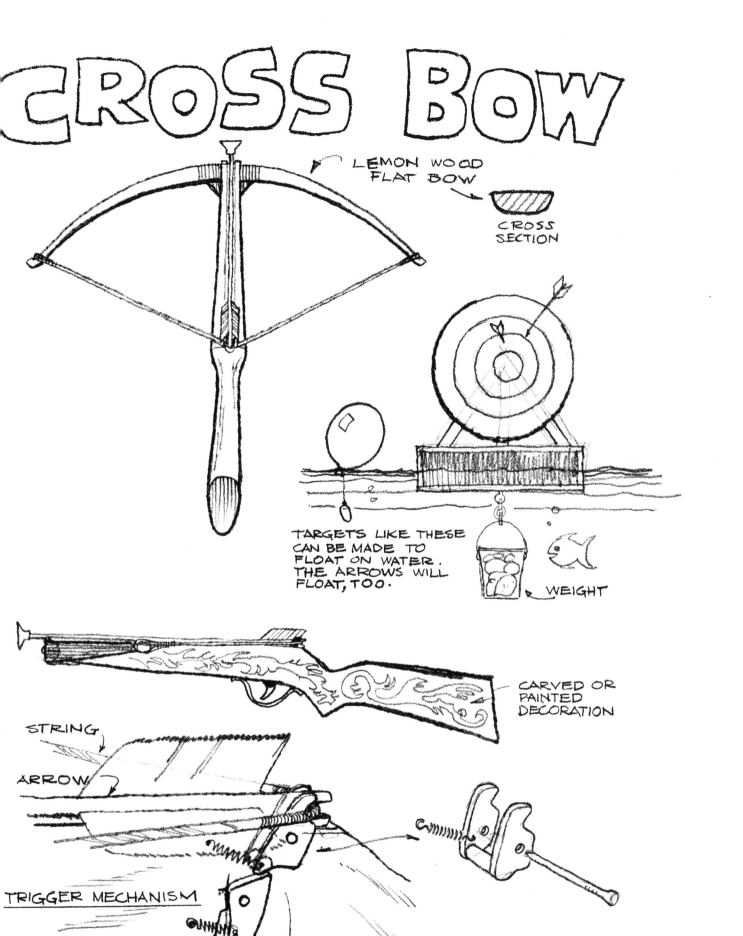

LEMON WOOD FLAT BOW

CROSS SECTION

TARGETS LIKE THESE CAN BE MADE TO FLOAT ON WATER. THE ARROWS WILL FLOAT, TOO.

WEIGHT

CARVED OR PAINTED DECORATION

STRING

ARROW

TRIGGER MECHANISM

CANNON

CLEAN-OUT PLUG

5"

JOINTING COMPOUND

BELL

COUPLINGS

30"

BELL

BARREL OF CANNON MADE FROM BITUMINIZED-FIBER SEWER PIPE.

THIS CANNON IS A GOOD TOY FOR ANY BOY FROM SIX TO TWELVE. IT IS COMPLETELY HARMLESS AND IS DESIGNED TO SHOOT SOFT BALLS.

THE BARREL IS MADE FROM PIECES OF SEWER PIPE, ALL OF WHICH YOU CAN FIND AT YOUR LOCAL PLUMBING SUPPLIER OR MAIL ORDER CATALOG FOR ABOUT FIVE DOLLARS.

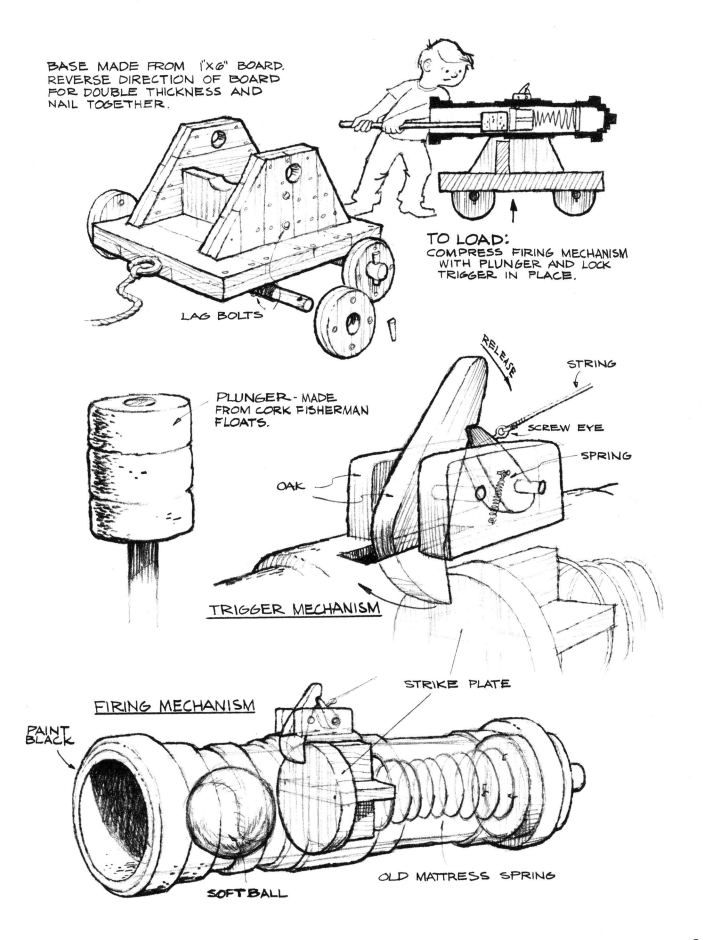

BASE MADE FROM 1"×6" BOARD.
REVERSE DIRECTION OF BOARD
FOR DOUBLE THICKNESS AND
NAIL TOGETHER.

TO LOAD:
COMPRESS FIRING MECHANISM
WITH PLUNGER AND LOCK
TRIGGER IN PLACE.

LAG BOLTS

PLUNGER - MADE
FROM CORK FISHERMAN
FLOATS.

RELEASE

STRING

SCREW EYE

SPRING

OAK

TRIGGER MECHANISM

STRIKE PLATE

FIRING MECHANISM

PAINT
BLACK

SOFTBALL

OLD MATTRESS SPRING

Horse

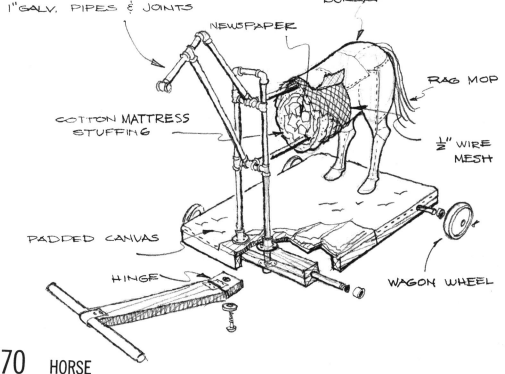

1" GALV. PIPES & JOINTS

NEWSPAPER

BURLAP

RAG MOP

COTTON MATTRESS STUFFING

½" WIRE MESH

PADDED CANVAS

HINGE

WAGON WHEEL

THIS HORSE CAN BE A LOT OF FUN FOR BOY FROM THE AGE EIGHT TO TWELVE. ALTHOUGH THE HORSE STRUCTUR CAN BE MADE OF WOO IT WILL LAST A LOT LONGER IF MADE WIT PIPE AS SHOWN AT LE

CARE SHOULD BE TA TO PROVIDE A SOFT COVERING BELOW TH HORSE IN CASE THE RIDER SHOULD FALL, KEEP WHEELS WIDE AND LOW TO THE GROUND TO PREVENT HORSE FROM TIPPIN OVER.

Pirate's Ship

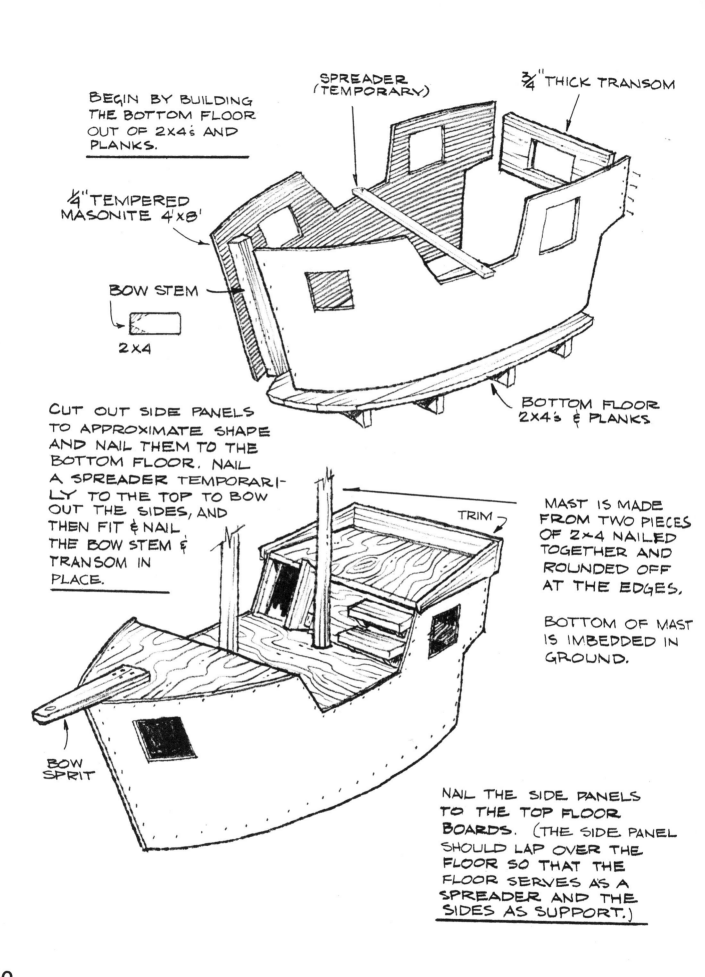

BEGIN BY BUILDING THE BOTTOM FLOOR OUT OF 2×4's AND PLANKS.

SPREADER (TEMPORARY)

¾" THICK TRANSOM

¼" TEMPERED MASONITE 4'×8'

BOW STEM

2×4

BOTTOM FLOOR 2×4's & PLANKS

CUT OUT SIDE PANELS TO APPROXIMATE SHAPE AND NAIL THEM TO THE BOTTOM FLOOR. NAIL A SPREADER TEMPORARILY TO THE TOP TO BOW OUT THE SIDES, AND THEN FIT & NAIL THE BOW STEM & TRANSOM IN PLACE.

TRIM

MAST IS MADE FROM TWO PIECES OF 2×4 NAILED TOGETHER AND ROUNDED OFF AT THE EDGES.

BOTTOM OF MAST IS IMBEDDED IN GROUND.

BOW SPRIT

NAIL THE SIDE PANELS TO THE TOP FLOOR BOARDS. (THE SIDE PANEL SHOULD LAP OVER THE FLOOR SO THAT THE FLOOR SERVES AS A SPREADER AND THE SIDES AS SUPPORT.)

Pirate's Ship
CONSTRUCTION DETAILS

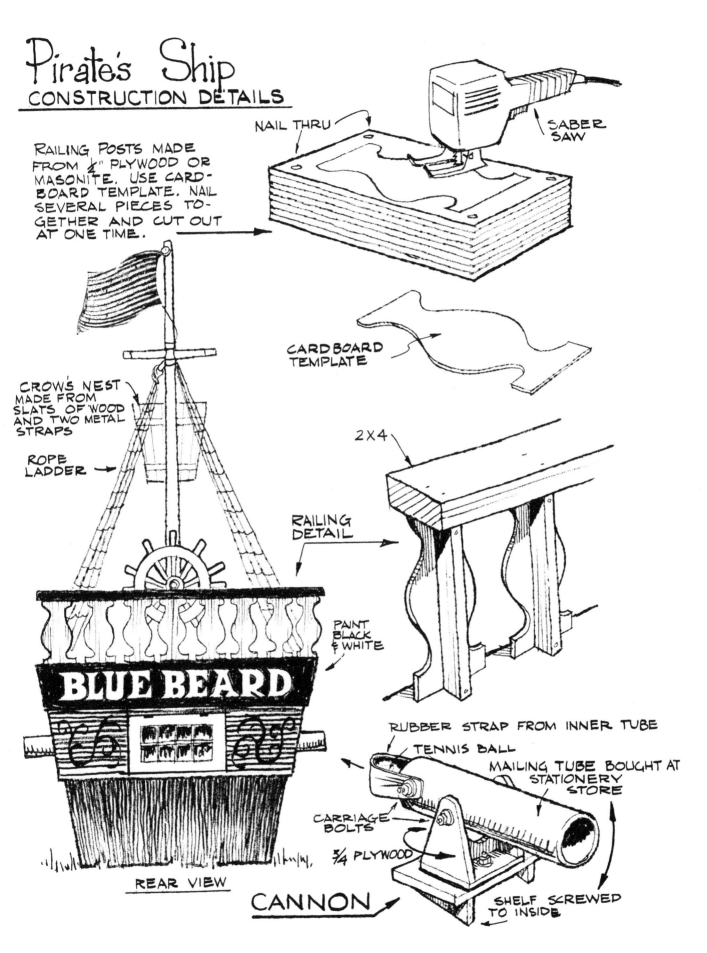

RAILING POSTS MADE FROM ½" PLYWOOD OR MASONITE. USE CARDBOARD TEMPLATE. NAIL SEVERAL PIECES TOGETHER AND CUT OUT AT ONE TIME.

NAIL THRU

SABER SAW

CROW'S NEST MADE FROM SLATS OF WOOD AND TWO METAL STRAPS

ROPE LADDER →

CARDBOARD TEMPLATE

RAILING DETAIL

2 X 4

PAINT BLACK & WHITE

BLUE BEARD

REAR VIEW

RUBBER STRAP FROM INNER TUBE

TENNIS BALL

MAILING TUBE BOUGHT AT STATIONERY STORE

CARRIAGE BOLTS

¾ PLYWOOD

SHELF SCREWED TO INSIDE

CANNON →

TREASURE CHEST

MAP

DRAW MAP WITH BROWN INK ON OLD YELLOW PAPER. CAREFULLY BROWN THE EDGES BY HOLDING PAPER OVER OPEN FLAME. SEAL MAP WITH RED CANDLE WAX. HIDE MAP IN SECRET PLACE.

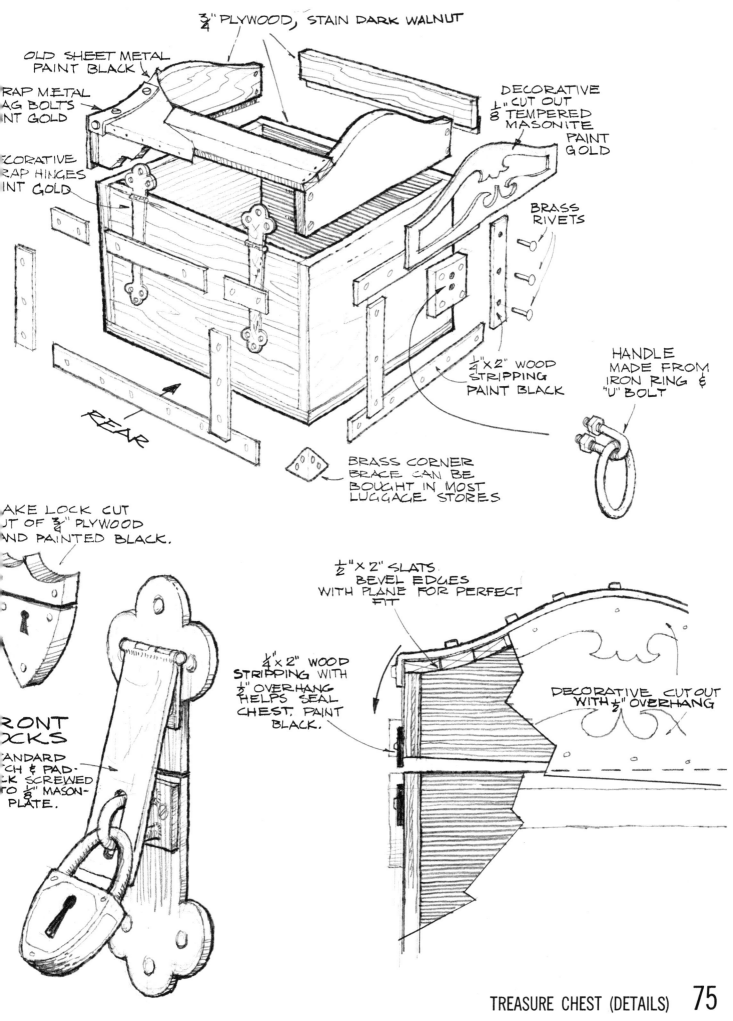

¾" PLYWOOD, STAIN DARK WALNUT

OLD SHEET METAL
PAINT BLACK

RAP METAL
AG BOLTS
NT GOLD

CORATIVE
RAP HINGES
NT GOLD

DECORATIVE
⅛" CUT OUT
TEMPERED
MASONITE
PAINT
GOLD

BRASS
RIVETS

½"X 2" WOOD
STRIPPING
PAINT BLACK

REAR

BRASS CORNER
BRACE CAN BE
BOUGHT IN MOST
LUGGAGE STORES

HANDLE
MADE FROM
IRON RING &
"U" BOLT

AKE LOCK CUT
JT OF ¾" PLYWOOD
ND PAINTED BLACK.

½" X 2" SLATS.
BEVEL EDGES
WITH PLANE FOR PERFECT
FIT

¼" X 2" WOOD
STRIPPING WITH
½" OVERHANG
HELPS SEAL
CHEST. PAINT
BLACK.

DECORATIVE CUT OUT
WITH ½" OVERHANG

RONT
CKS

ANDARD
CH & PAD-
K SCREWED
TO ⅛" MASON-
PLATE.

BRONCO

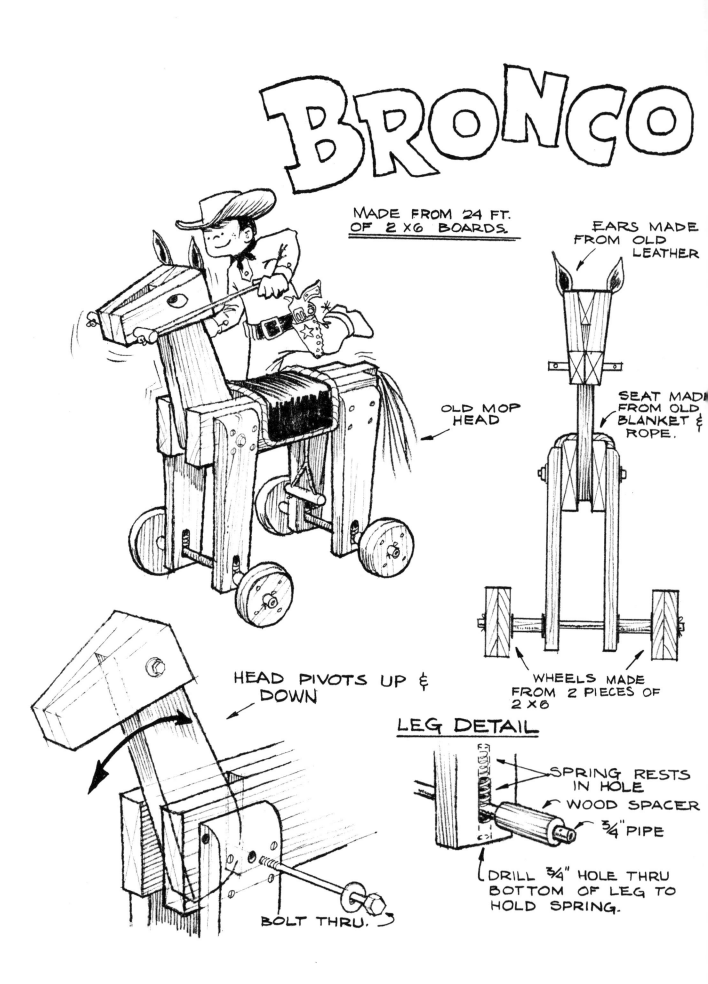

MADE FROM 24 FT. OF 2 X6 BOARDS.

EARS MADE FROM OLD LEATHER

OLD MOP HEAD

SEAT MADE FROM OLD BLANKET & ROPE.

WHEELS MADE FROM 2 PIECES OF 2 X6

HEAD PIVOTS UP & DOWN

BOLT THRU.

LEG DETAIL

SPRING RESTS IN HOLE

WOOD SPACER

¾" PIPE

DRILL ¾" HOLE THRU BOTTOM OF LEG TO HOLD SPRING.

COVERED WAGON

THE COVERED WAGON IS AN ANTIQUE AND IF CAREFULLY CONSTRUCTED, SHOULD BE A SOURCE OF PRIDE FOR BOTH FATHER & SON. MEASURES WERE TAKEN IN THIS DESIGN TO SIMPLIFY CONSTRUCTION. SINCE THE WHEELS ARE THE HARDEST PART TO MAKE, IF YOU CAN FIND ANY OLD WAGON WHEELS IN A LOCAL ANTIQUE STORE, YOU WILL SAVE YOURSELF A GREAT DEAL OF TIME.

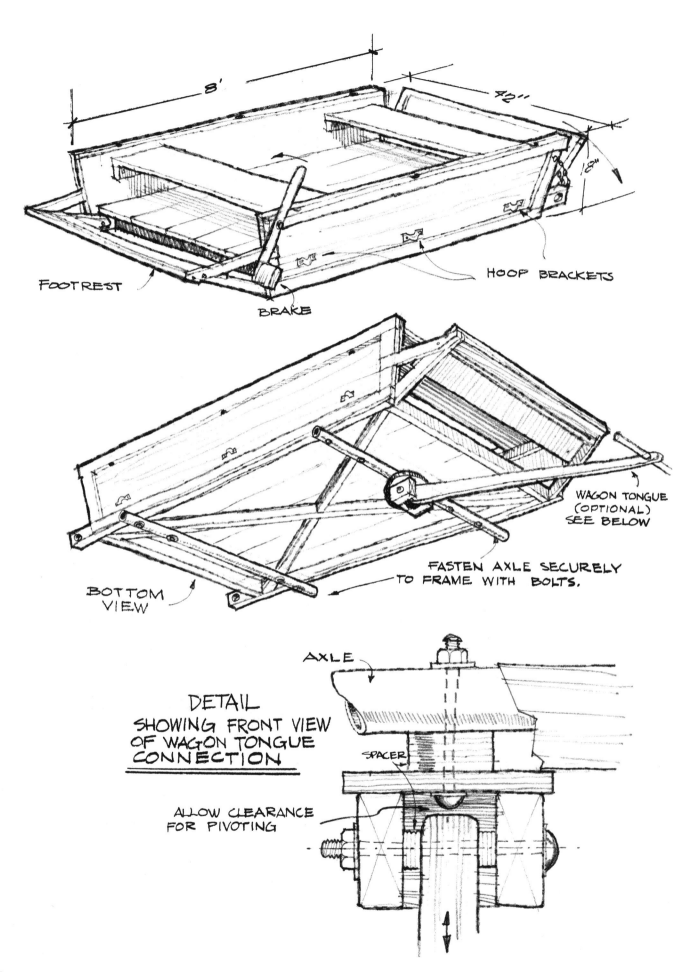

8'

42"

8"

FOOTREST

BRAKE

HOOP BRACKETS

BOTTOM VIEW

WAGON TONGUE (OPTIONAL) SEE BELOW

FASTEN AXLE SECURELY TO FRAME WITH BOLTS.

DETAIL
SHOWING FRONT VIEW OF WAGON TONGUE CONNECTION

AXLE

SPACER

ALLOW CLEARANCE FOR PIVOTING

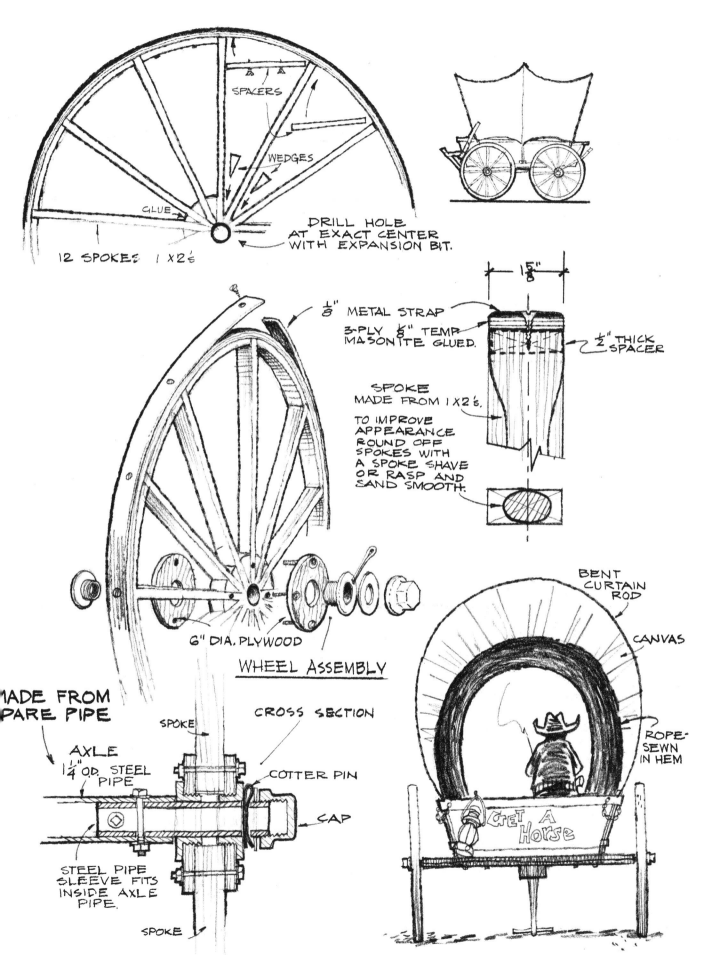

SPACERS

WEDGES

GLUE

12 SPOKES 1 X 2's

DRILL HOLE AT EXACT CENTER WITH EXPANSION BIT.

$\frac{5}{8}$"

$\frac{1}{8}$" METAL STRAP

3-PLY $\frac{1}{8}$" TEMP MASONITE GLUED.

$\frac{1}{2}$" THICK SPACER

SPOKE MADE FROM 1 X 2's.

TO IMPROVE APPEARANCE ROUND OFF SPOKES WITH A SPOKE SHAVE OR RASP AND SAND SMOOTH.

6" DIA. PLYWOOD

WHEEL ASSEMBLY

MADE FROM SPARE PIPE

SPOKE

CROSS SECTION

AXLE 1$\frac{1}{4}$" O.D. STEEL PIPE

COTTER PIN

CAP

STEEL PIPE SLEEVE FITS INSIDE AXLE PIPE.

SPOKE

BENT CURTAIN ROD

CANVAS

ROPE- SEWN IN HEM

Get A Horse

COVERED WAGON (DETAILS) 79

Scooter

SCRAP WOOD

OLD SODA BOX

SCOOTERS LIKE THESE ARE MADE BY KIDS IN CITIES ALL OVER UNITED STATES.

OLD HINGES SERVE AS BRACKETS

ALTERNATE-STYLE SCOOTER MADE FROM OLD SODA BOX. HAS SPECIAL STORAGE COMPARTMENT.

TWO HALVES OF OLD ROLLER SKATE SCREWED TO BOTTOM OF 2 X 4.

FASTEN FRONT SKATE WITH ON BOLT SO WHEEL CAN TURN SLIGHTL

Wishing Well

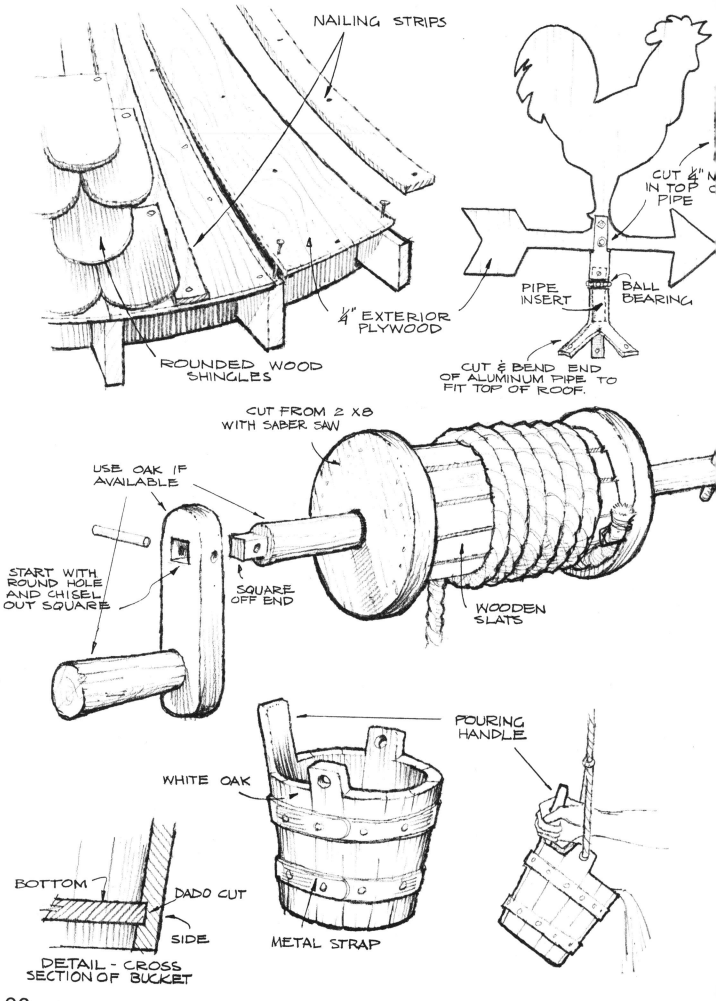

NAILING STRIPS

¼" EXTERIOR
PLYWOOD

ROUNDED WOOD
SHINGLES

CUT ¼" N
IN TOP O
PIPE

PIPE
INSERT

BALL
BEARING

CUT & BEND END
OF ALUMINUM PIPE TO
FIT TOP OF ROOF.

CUT FROM 2 x 8
WITH SABER SAW

USE OAK IF
AVAILABLE

START WITH
ROUND HOLE
AND CHISEL
OUT SQUARE

SQUARE
OFF END

WOODEN
SLATS

POURING
HANDLE

WHITE OAK

BOTTOM

DADO CUT

SIDE

DETAIL - CROSS
SECTION OF BUCKET

METAL STRAP

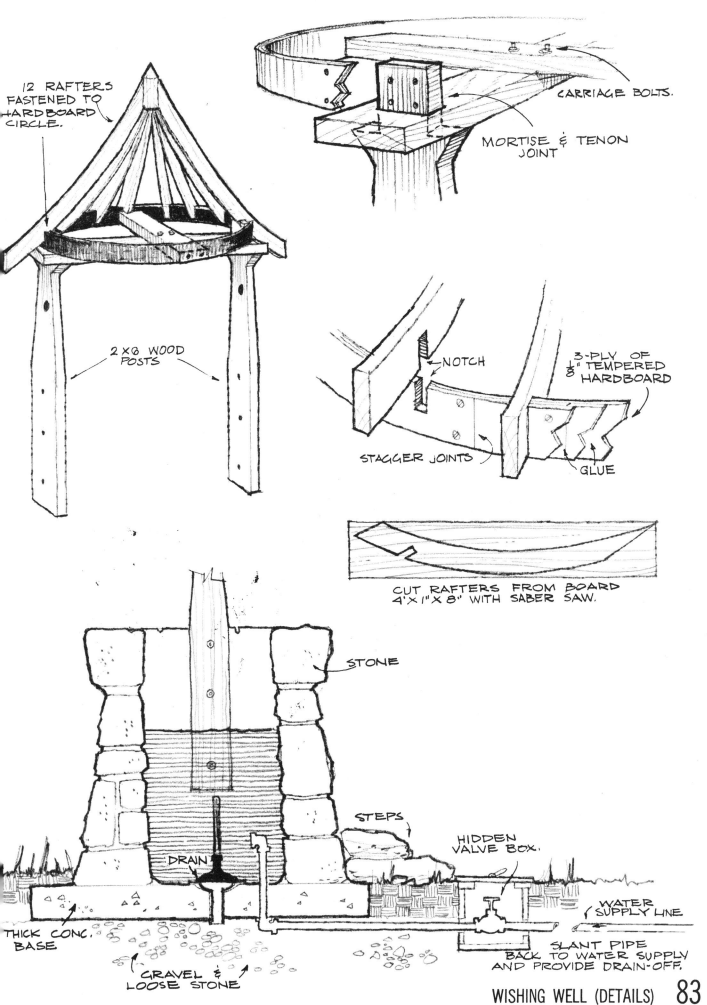

12 RAFTERS FASTENED TO HARDBOARD CIRCLE.

CARRIAGE BOLTS.

MORTISE & TENON JOINT

2 X 8 WOOD POSTS

NOTCH

3-PLY OF $\frac{1}{8}$" TEMPERED HARDBOARD

STAGGER JOINTS

GLUE

CUT RAFTERS FROM BOARD 4' X 1" X 8" WITH SABER SAW.

STONE

STEPS

HIDDEN VALVE BOX.

DRAIN

THICK CONC. BASE

GRAVEL & LOOSE STONE

WATER SUPPLY LINE

SLANT PIPE BACK TO WATER SUPPLY AND PROVIDE DRAIN-OFF.

WISHING WELL (DETAILS)

Jungle Drum

SAW LOG IN HALF

$1\frac{1}{2}"$

LEAVE ONE END CLOSE

FILL SCREW HOLE WITH DOWELS

GLUE & SCREW

FIND A BIG LOG - AS THICK AS POSSIBLE - AND SAW IT OFF AT 3 TO 4 FT. STRIP OFF THE BARK AND SAW IT IN HALF. HOLLOW OUT EACH HALF WITH A CHISEL AND JOIN THEM TOGETHER WITH GLUE AND SCREWS. SUSPEND DRUM FROM TREE WITH TWO ROPES.

Möbius Strip

THIS SIMPLE TRICK WILL AMAZE YOUR FRIENDS

CUT A 1" PIECE OFF A LETTER SIZED
PIECE OF PAPER.

1"

TWIST ONE END OF
THE STRIP AND
GLUE OR TAPE
IT TO THE OTHER
END.

MÖBIUS
← STRIP

Tape or Glue

CUT IT LENGTHWISE
DOWN THE MIDDLE
AND YOU WILL GET
TWO LOOPS.....
OR DO YOU ???

TRY IT...

THEN TRY CUTTING
IT LENGTHWISE AGAIN
AND SEE WHAT YOU GET.

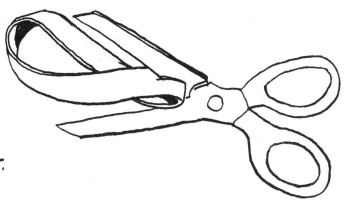

THIS SIMPLE PHENOMENON HAS PUZZELED
MATHEMATICIANS AND PHYSICISTS FOR YEARS.

☆☆☆ THE MÖBIUS STRIP HAS ONLY ONE
SIDE AND ONLY ONE EDGE!!!

RAILROAD ENGINE

A RAILROAD ENGINE LIKE THIS IS NOT AS HARD TO MAKE AS IT MIGHT APPEAR. THE FRONT-END CYLINDER IS A PAPER PACKING BARREL. THE SMOKE STACK IS MADE FROM AN OLD WASTE PAPER BASKET AND A LAMP SHADE. TAKE THE WHEELS FROM OLD BICYCLES, TRICYCLES OR BABY CARRIAGES. ADD A MASONITE OR PLYWOOD COVER PLATE OVER THE WHEELS AND PAINT ON BLACK SPOKES. IF DESIRED THE ENGINE CAN BE RUN ON A TRACK OVER A PREDETERMINED COURSE (A SECTION OF THE TRACK IS SHOWN AT THE BOTTOM OF THE NEXT PAGE.)

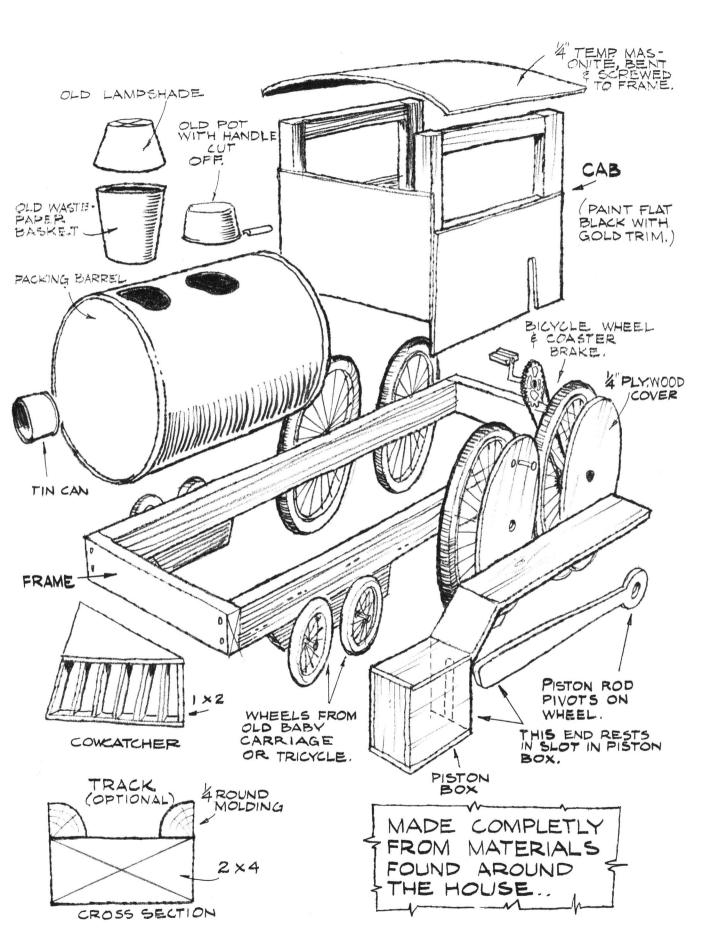

OLD LAMPSHADE

OLD POT WITH HANDLE CUT OFF.

OLD WASTE-PAPER BASKET

PACKING BARREL

TIN CAN

¼" TEMP MASONITE, BENT & SCREWED TO FRAME.

CAB
(PAINT FLAT BLACK WITH GOLD TRIM.)

BICYCLE WHEEL & COASTER BRAKE.

¼" PLYWOOD COVER

FRAME

1 × 2

COWCATCHER

WHEELS FROM OLD BABY CARRIAGE OR TRICYCLE.

PISTON ROD PIVOTS ON WHEEL.

THIS END RESTS IN SLOT IN PISTON BOX.

PISTON BOX

TRACK (OPTIONAL)

¼ ROUND MOLDING

2 × 4

CROSS SECTION

MADE COMPLETLY FROM MATERIALS FOUND AROUND THE HOUSE..

RAILROAD ENGINE (DETAILS) 87

JokeBox

This innocent looking box holds a surprise for any curious person opening it. Written on the outside are the word "WORLD'S MOST DANGEROUS ANIMAL". When opened, the box reveals a dark cage with grass in it. On closer inspection the observer sees HIMSELF reflected in a mirror.

Once the joke has run it's course, the box can be used as a mail box or a place to leave messages.

PAD & PENCIL

MAIL

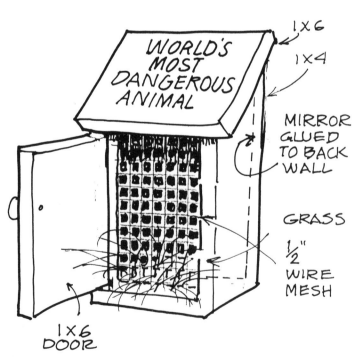

WORLD'S MOST DANGEROUS ANIMAL

1X6

1X4

MIRROR GLUED TO BACK WALL

GRASS

½" WIRE MESH

1X6 DOOR

Scooter from a Skate Board

An old skateboard can be converted into a terrific scooter by adding just a few pieces of wood.

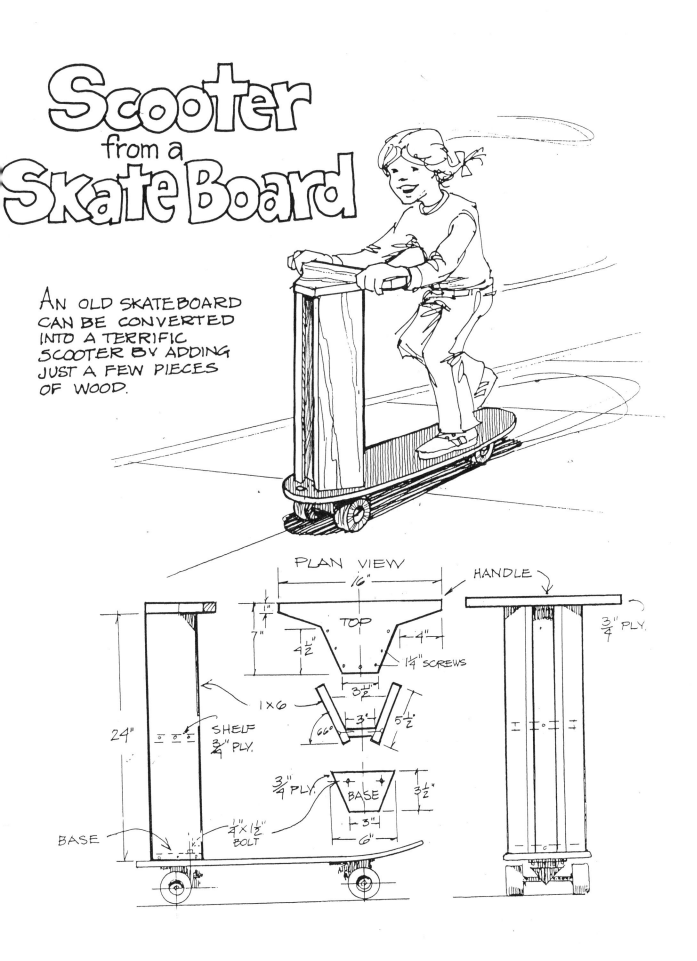

PLAN VIEW

16"

TOP

1"

7"

4½"

4"

1¼" SCREWS

1×6

3½"

3"

5½"

66°

SHELF ¾" PLY.

24"

¾" PLY.

BASE

3½"

3"

6"

BASE

¼" × 1½" BOLT

HANDLE

¾" PLY.

TANK

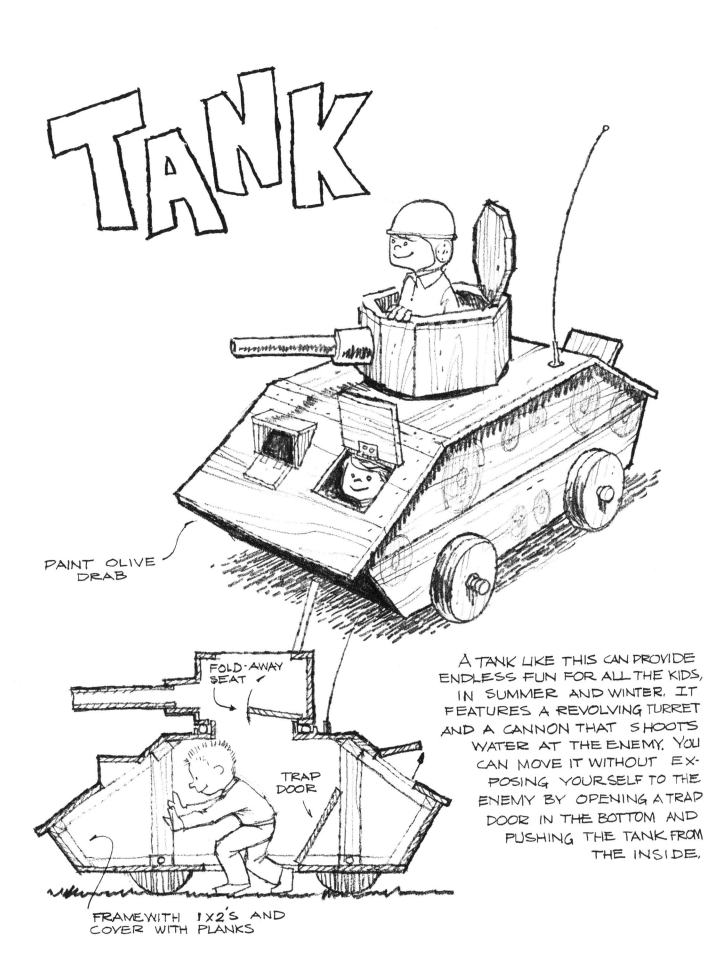

PAINT OLIVE DRAB

FOLD-AWAY SEAT

TRAP DOOR

FRAME WITH 1x2's AND COVER WITH PLANKS

A TANK LIKE THIS CAN PROVIDE ENDLESS FUN FOR ALL THE KIDS, IN SUMMER AND WINTER. IT FEATURES A REVOLVING TURRET AND A CANNON THAT SHOOTS WATER AT THE ENEMY. YOU CAN MOVE IT WITHOUT EXPOSING YOURSELF TO THE ENEMY BY OPENING A TRAP DOOR IN THE BOTTOM AND PUSHING THE TANK FROM THE INSIDE.

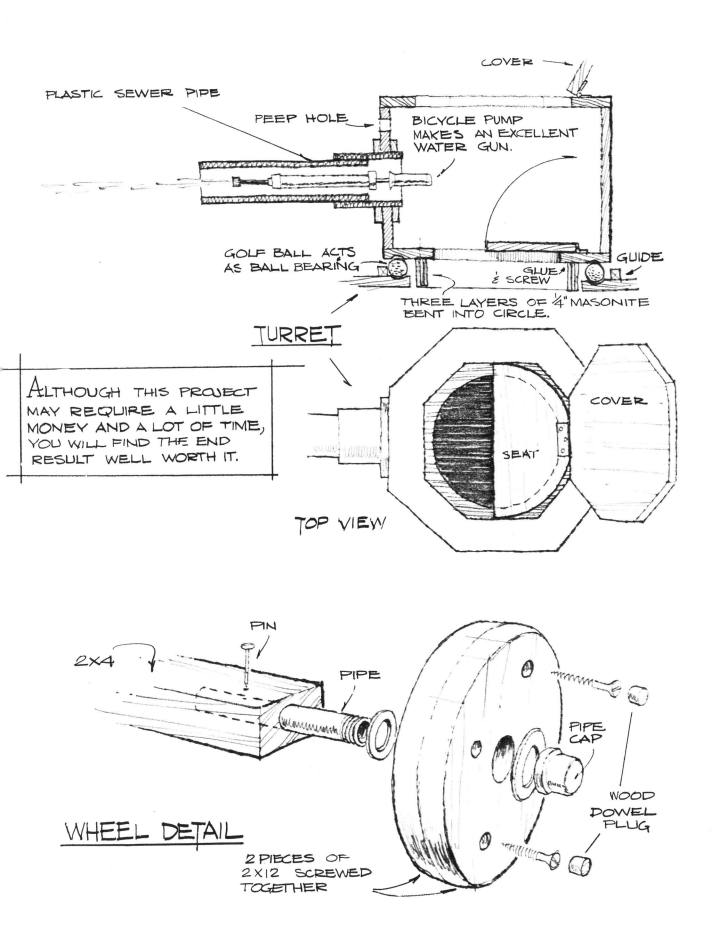

PLASTIC SEWER PIPE

PEEP HOLE

COVER

BICYCLE PUMP MAKES AN EXCELLENT WATER GUN.

GOLF BALL ACTS AS BALL BEARING

GLUE & SCREW

GUIDE

THREE LAYERS OF ¼" MASONITE BENT INTO CIRCLE.

TURRET

ALTHOUGH THIS PROJECT MAY REQUIRE A LITTLE MONEY AND A LOT OF TIME, YOU WILL FIND THE END RESULT WELL WORTH IT.

SEAT

COVER

TOP VIEW

PIN

2X4

PIPE

PIPE CAP

WOOD DOWEL PLUG

WHEEL DETAIL

2 PIECES OF 2X12 SCREWED TOGETHER

SPACE SHIP

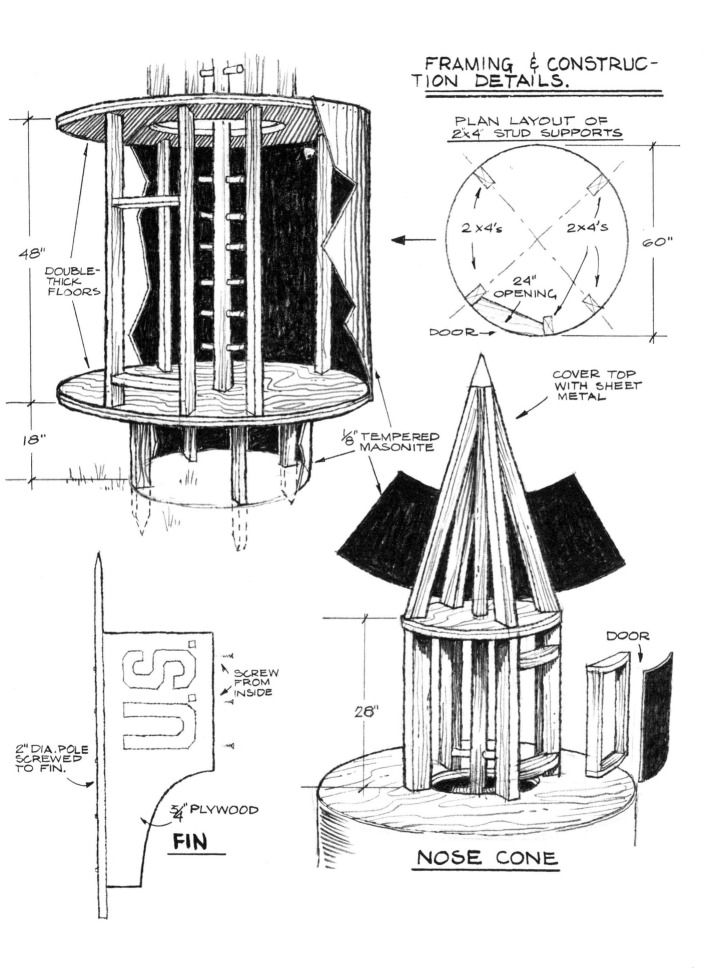

FRAMING & CONSTRUCTION DETAILS.

48" — DOUBLE-THICK FLOORS

18"

PLAN LAYOUT OF 2"x4" STUD SUPPORTS

2 x 4's   2 x 4's

24" OPENING

DOOR →

60"

⅛" TEMPERED MASONITE

COVER TOP WITH SHEET METAL

DOOR →

28"

NOSE CONE

SCREW FROM INSIDE

2" DIA. POLE SCREWED TO FIN.

¾" PLYWOOD

FIN

U.S.

AIRPLANE

NOSE MADE FROM OLD PAIL.

WINDSHIELD MADE FROM CURTAIN RODS.

TAIL & WINGS MADE FROM 3/4" PLYWOOD

SLANT THIS PANEL BACK TO TRAILING EDGE OF TAIL.

SIMPLE BOX 1/2" PLYWOOD

1 X 2 STRUT

PROP SHAPED FROM 2 X 4

LEMONADE STAND

Lemonade 3¢

CANVAS ROOF
SUPPORTED BY RODS

PLASTIC TUBE

CASH BOX — MONEY
DROPS THRU SLOTS
INTO DRAWER.

1¢ 5¢ 10¢ 2

DRAWER

CUPS

NOTCH
(CROSS SECTION)

2×2

VALVE

TOP VIEW

Traveling Zoo

ZOO →

tiger ape snake

5¢

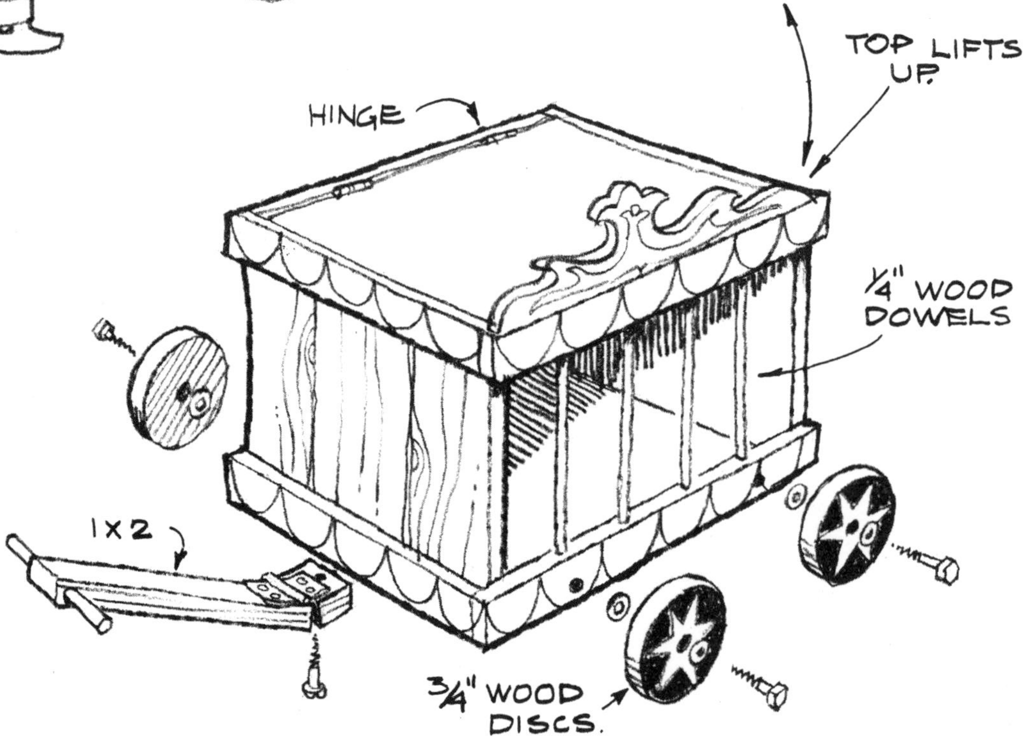

TOP LIFTS UP.

HINGE

¼" WOOD DOWELS

1×2

¾" WOOD DISCS.